Advance Praise for
They Will Inherit the Earth

"In these heartfelt essays, John Dear navigates our most challenging environmental issues with simple decency, purposeful compassion and an unswerving commitment to justice."

—Michael Brune,
executive director, Sierra Club

"This is a remarkable testimony summing up a remarkable life: nonviolence is our greatest tool, and here you see it wielded with kindness, firmness, and skill."

—Bill McKibben, author,
EAARTH: Making a Life on a Tough New Planet,
and founder of 350.org

"If you want to know what *Laudato Si'* and the Sermon on the Mount look like up close and personal, as a life of consistent nonviolence, John Dear is your guide and *They Will Inherit the Earth* is your text. I strongly recommend it."

—Larry Rasmussen,
Reinhold Niebuhr Professor Emeritus
of Social Ethics, Union Theological Seminary,
New York City

"John Dear is an extraordinarily lucid writer on peace and nonviolence. If we are to save this world from destruction, we need to wake up and start building peace and nonviolence."

—Arun Gandhi, author, activist,
and lecturer on Gandhian nonviolence

"In the spirit of Martin Luther King Jr.'s and Mahatma Gandhi's audacious visions of nonviolence, Father John Dear's powerful new book is a lyrical invocation that will help transform our conflict-riven world through acts of compassion and pilgrimages of peacemaking. *They Will Inherit the Earth* is that rare work that combines the author's own remarkable life of fearless love as a peace pilgrim with a transcultural portrait of individuals around the globe who are actively trying to ward off ecological and political calamity by promoting unity over conflict, and compassion over revenge. This brave new book is a numinous guide to a brave new — and peaceful — world."

**—Phil Cousineau,
author, *The Art of Pilgrimage***

"Calling us to practice 'eschatological nonviolence' in our relationships with a threatened planet *They Will Inherit the Earth* creates a new frame for the ecological challenges of the 21st century and makes a significant contribution to a deeper understanding of Gospel nonviolence. In *Laudato Si'*, Pope Francis insists that the effects of our encounter with Jesus Christ become evident in our relationship with the world around us. John Dear helps us think about that challenge in a new way. This is an important book to read and to ponder, but even more to live."

**—Marie Dennis, co-president
Pax Christi International**

"With his message and his lived example, John Dear demonstrates how we can maintain our humanity as we grapple with the greatest crisis facing our civilization."

**—Tim DeChristopher,
co-founder of peacefuluprising.org**

They Will Inherit the Earth

Peace and Nonviolence
in a Time of Climate Change

John Dear

ORBIS BOOKS
Maryknoll, New York

Second Printing, April 2018

Founded in 1970, Orbis Books endeavors to publish works that enlighten the mind, nourish the spirit, and challenge the conscience. The publishing arm of the Maryknoll Fathers and Brothers, Orbis seeks to explore the global dimensions of the Christian faith and mission, to invite dialogue with diverse cultures and religious traditions, and to serve the cause of reconciliation and peace. The books published reflect the views of their authors and do not represent the official position of the Maryknoll Society. To learn more about Maryknoll and Orbis Books, please visit our website at www.maryknollsociety.org.

Library of Congress Cataloging-in-Publication Data

Names: Dear, John, 1959- author.
Title: They will inherit the earth : peace and nonviolence in a time of climate change / John Dear.
Description: Maryknoll, NY : Orbis Books, 2018.
Identifiers: LCCN 2017035703 (print) | LCCN 2017046987 (ebook) | ISBN 9781608337309 (e-book) | ISBN 9781626982642 (pbk.)
Subjects: LCSH: Nonviolence—Religious aspects—Christianity. | Peace—Religious aspects—Christianity. | Human ecology—Religious aspects—Christianity. | Ecotheology. | Climatic changes. | Sermon on the mount.
Classification: LCC BT736.6 (ebook) | LCC BT736.6 .D427 2018 (print) | DDC 241/.697—dc23
LC record available at https://lccn.loc.gov/2017035703

For Renea Roberts and Mat Crimmins,
Friends, Neighbors, and Peacemakers

Also by John Dear

Disarming the Heart
Jean Donovan and the Call to Discipleship
It's a Sin to Build a Nuclear Weapon: Writings of Richard McSorley (ed.)
Our God Is Nonviolent
Oscar Romero and the Nonviolent Struggle for Justice
Seeds of Nonviolence
The God of Peace: Toward a Theology of Nonviolence
The Sacrament of Civil Disobedience
Peace behind Bars
Apostle of Peace: Essays in Honor of Daniel Berrigan (ed.)
Jesus the Rebel
The Road to Peace: Writings of Henri Nouwen (ed.)
The Sound of Listening
The Vision of Peace: Writings of Mairead Maguire (ed.)
And the Risen Bread: Selected Poems of Daniel Berrigan (ed.)
Living Peace
Mohandas Gandhi: Essential Writings (ed.)
Mary of Nazareth, Prophet of Peace
The Questions of Jesus
Transfiguration
You Will Be My Witnesses
The Advent of Peace
A Persistent Peace: An Autobiography
Put Down Your Sword
Daniel Berrigan: Essential Writings (ed.)
Lazarus, Come Forth!
The Nonviolent Life
Walking the Way
Thomas Merton: Peacemaker
The Beatitudes of Peace
Radical Prayers

The world is charged with the grandeur of God.

—Gerard Manley Hopkins

Will you teach your children what we have taught our children? That the earth is our mother? What befalls the earth befalls all the sons and daughters of the earth. This we know: the earth does not belong to humans; humans belong to the earth. All things are connected like the blood that unites us all. Humans did not weave the web of life; they are merely a strand in it. Whatever humans do to the web, they do to themselves. One thing we know: our God is also your God. The earth is precious to God and to harm the earth is to heap contempt on its Creator.

—Chief Seattle

We should deal with nature the same way we deal with ourselves: nonviolently. Human beings and nature are inseparable. Just as we should not harm ourselves, we should not harm nature. To harm nature is to harm ourselves, and vice versa.

—Thich Nhat Hanh

All peoples of the earth, all men and women of good will—all of us must raise our voices in defense of these two precious gifts: peace and nature.

—Pope Francis

We will survive our personal losses; they are ultimately what gives us our voice. . . . But the losses of the larger world, call it the pain of the grieving Earth, threaten our sanity and survival. These losses of species and landscapes, we must face together with an open heart. Attention is our prayer. Engagement is our vow.

—Terry Tempest Williams

We can't let them burn down the planet!

—Philip Berrigan

Contents

Introduction

I've spent my life chasing an idea—the idea of nonviolence. When I was young, I noticed that the greatest people in modern history—beginning with Mohandas Gandhi, Dorothy Day, and Martin Luther King Jr.—gave every moment of their lives to nonviolence. I decided that if that's what our greatest people did with their lives, that's what I should do, too.

For nearly four decades now, I've pursued the ideal of nonviolence around the nation and the world. I've walked through the war zones of Israel, Palestine, El Salvador, Nicaragua, Guatemala, Colombia, Haiti, Iraq, Egypt, the Philippines, South Africa, and Afghanistan; been arrested some eighty times in nonviolent civil disobedience against war and injustice; spent time in soup kitchens, homeless shelters, and jails across the United States; and stood before a million people in crowded churches around the nation and the world struggling to articulate and lift up the vision of creative nonviolence.

One thing I've learned is that if you are going to stand up publicly every day of your life and advocate nonviolence, someone will inevitably stand up and justify violence whether through the just war theory, the latest U.S. war, the need to have a gun or a bomb, or the broken human condition of violence. In other words, I've spent nearly every day of my life trying to talk people out of killing others, waging war, or quietly supporting the culture of violence. It's been a long, difficult trip, but as my friend Daniel Berrigan once said to me, at least it hasn't been dull.

My life is a long pilgrimage of peace, a pilgrimage of nonviolence. After every trip, every arrest, every talk, I've returned home over the last fifteen years to my mountaintop hermitage

1

on a remote mesa in New Mexico, where I look out at sixty miles of my own Southwest paradise. I take in the beauty of the surrounding landscape, breathe in the peace of creation, open the gospel, sit in the presence of the Creator, and listen again to the words of peace.

Over the decades, I have witnessed the destruction we humans have done to Mother Earth and her creatures. I've read about catastrophic climate change and experienced the changes—the droughts, the strange weather, the extreme fires and tornadoes and rainfall—in the Southwest and elsewhere. I grieve for Mother Earth and the creatures who die because of our systemic greed, violence, and destructive habits. But I never made or felt the connection between my vision of nonviolence and the ongoing destruction of Mother Earth.

Until now.

One day, while sitting in my house studying the Sermon on the Mount, I saw it right there in front of me. "Blessed are the meek," Jesus says in the Beatitudes. Thomas Merton wrote that "meekness" is the biblical word for nonviolence. "Blessed are the nonviolent," Jesus is saying, as if he were an ancient Gandhi, an ancient Dorothy Day, an ancient Martin Luther King Jr. "They will inherit the earth."

There it is. Blessed are the meek, the gentle, the nonviolent—they will inherit the earth.

A life of nonviolence leads to oneness with creation and her creatures.

A life of violence, of course, leads to an abrupt discord with creation. In a time of permanent warfare, nuclear weapons, and catastrophic climate change, the message couldn't be clearer. The God of peace, the nonviolent Jesus, and his Holy Spirit call us to practice nonviolence. In that way, we'll renounce and stop our environmental destruction, tend our Garden of Eden together, and restore creation to its rightful peace. In the process, we will discover peace with one another and all the creatures.

Here on my mesa mountaintop, surrounded by coyotes, jackrabbits, and juniper, it all came home. I was inheriting the earth. I was one with creation. I had entered the promised land. A life of nonviolence had led me to this geography of peace.

More, this is the journey we are all called to live, to make the connection between active nonviolence and oneness with creation, so that we all might dwell peacefully in this paradise. In that moment, I saw not just the vision of peace and non-violence, but the vision of a new creation, where we all live as one in peace with one another, Mother Earth and her glorious creatures. It's that vision of peace, nonviolence, and the new creation, the vision of the promised land before us, the practice of proactive nonviolence, that offers a way out of environmental destruction, as well as permanent war, corporate greed, systemic racism, and extreme poverty.

All we have to do is open our eyes to the reality of creation before us, to be present to it, to take it in and honor it, and welcome its gift of peace—and do so within the boundaries of nonviolence. In that present moment of peace, a new creation is offered to us once again.

Just as the vision of peace guided me to speak out over the years, especially after September 11 and the start of the U.S. wars on Afghanistan and Iraq, so too a vision of creation inspires me to speak out against our destructive environmental policies, systems, and habits so that Mother Earth and her creatures might survive, so that future generations might have a chance.

We need not be blind any longer. We can reclaim this vision of peace for ourselves, Mother Earth, and her creatures. We can go forward in peace to make peace with creation and welcome a new future of peace at one with all creation. The choice is ours. All we have to do is take the next step on the path of peace.

CHAPTER 1

The Vision of Peace in New York City

On the morning of September 11, 2001, I was having breakfast atop the Park Lane hotel with my parents on Central Park South, looking out over the green trees and lawns of Central Park. It was a stunning, clear blue day. We had reservations for breakfast at Windows on the World on the top of the Second World Trade Center Tower for that morning, but a few days before, my parents changed their mind to be closer to where I lived, in a community of priests on the Upper West Side, right on Broadway.

As soon as we heard the news, my parents left town. I headed downtown, to see if I could volunteer my help. Because the subways, roads, and bridges were shut down, I found myself walking directly into a crowd of oncoming millions, all fleeing the pillar of gray and pink smoke that climbed into the blue sky. At one point, military jets swooped down over Manhattan. The fear was palpable. No one knew whether or not more attacks were on the way. Still I walked on, into the terrified millions, closer to the towering smoke.

I stopped at Twelfth Street and waited outside St. Vincent's hospital with other chaplains to offer pastoral care to the wounded when they arrived. Doctors, nurses, and a few other chaplains lined Twelfth Street with stretchers and wheelchairs, waiting for the ambulances.

They never came. At nightfall, I headed back up Broadway to my community of priests.

At 5 a.m. the following Thursday morning, I set off again, this time for the New York Armory on Lexington Avenue, which the mayor opened as a temporary assistance center for those who had relatives missing in the World Trade Center Towers attacks. Ten thousand people lined the center of the road, waiting for the doors to open. I walked past them all, right into the building, and there met the Red Cross director of chaplains, a remarkable woman from Sacramento who was on call that month in case of a national emergency. She flew to New York on a military plane on Tuesday afternoon and immediately set to work establishing the Red Cross Family Assistance Center.

"Do you need any help?" I asked. "I'm Fr. John, a Catholic priest."

"Yes," she said. "Go stand over there in the corner. After we process everyone, we'll ask them if they want to speak to a chaplain, and we'll send them to you."

"But there are ten thousand people out there!" I said nervously.

"You'll do fine," she said with a smile.

"What do I do?" I asked.

"Just listen to them and be compassionate." With that, she smiled and walked away.

I took my place in the corner, and the first relative came forward. She cried, told me about her missing husband, and asked me to pray for her. And so I did.

So began three months of grief work with the victims of September 11. By the end of that day, after speaking with countless grieving New Yorkers, the woman from Sacramento came back over to me. "We've been watching you," she said. "We want you to be the coordinator of chaplains for the Family Assistance Center for the next few months. Can you do it?" I said yes and with that set off on a long journey of grief, compassion, and protest.

By Monday morning, the city had moved the Family Assistance Center into one of the massive convention halls used for fashion shows on the piers along West Fiftieth Street. I coordinated over six hundred chaplains from all faiths ministering to over fifty thousand direct family members of the victims—spouses, parents, or children. I also worked one or two days a week at Ground Zero itself, talking and praying with hundreds of rescue workers. It was exhausting, challenging, disturbing, and inspiring all at once. I met entire families, telling them that their loved one's body had been found; I prayed with all kinds of people and listened to their stories. At Ground Zero, I met scores of rescue workers. They would see me, in my black outfit and yellow hard hat, run down the seven-story pile of burning ruin, ask for a prayer and a blessing, and run back up in search of survivors.

All the while, my friends and I held weekly peace vigils around the city. We spoke against a retaliatory war, prayed for a miracle of peace, and distributed leaflets to passers-by in Union Square, Times Square, and Washington Square. At news of the impending U.S. bombing of Afghanistan, we organized a massive peace march and rally in Times Square on the first Saturday of October. Thousands marched, sang for peace, and protested the attack. The war began, but we continued to speak out for peace. For me, it was simply obedience to the gospel commandments to love my neighbors, in this case the wounded people of New York City, and to love my nation's enemies, the people of Afghanistan, Iraq, and elsewhere.

For decades, I had been speaking out, writing, lecturing, and preaching about peace. With September 11, the invitations poured in, and I accepted every one. I traveled the nation, speaking against war, urging more protests, advocating for a new culture of peace, and recommending the practice and methodology of active nonviolence that Gandhi and Dr. King taught. As the U.S. wars on Afghanistan and Iraq began, I did what I could to say No, to help mobilize national opposition to the war, and to advocate for nonviolent solutions to international conflict.

The insane suicidal attacks of September 11, 2001, were the natural consequence of years of U.S. military domination and warfare around the world. In the 1990s, the United States had bombed Iraq and imposed deadly sanctions that killed hundreds of thousands of people, mainly children. The United States funded the brutal Israeli occupation of the Palestinian people, which crushed and killed thousands. We had supported dictators around the world to hasten our global economic control and threatened everyone with nuclear weapons.

One day shortly after September 11, my friend Father Daniel Berrigan and I held a daylong retreat with our friends Shelley and Jim Douglass, longtime activists, Catholic Workers, and teachers of gospel nonviolence. We prayed together, read the Gospels, and reflected on the predicament of the moment. We knew we were in a time of great blindness, where no one could see a way forward except through war. We knew the forces of war and their media propaganda would use the September 11 attacks to further the agenda of global domination, to terrorize us all, sell more weapons, and seize the natural resources of other lands. We knew, too, that war never leads to peace, that war always leads to further wars, that war cannot stop terrorism because war is terrorism, and that war only serves the powers of corporate greed and global domination. But we also saw a way forward. We had a vision of peace. We saw the possibilities of nonviolence to resolve our national and global conflict. We realized once again that active nonviolence was the only way forward, the only hope for the world, the only methodological response to the crisis.

Together, we prayed for the strength to take the nonviolent Jesus at his word, to continue to teach nonviolence and to work to build up the global grassroots movement for a new culture of peace and nonviolence. We read what Jesus said in the Sermon on the Mount. "You have heard it said, 'An eye for an eye' and 'A tooth for a tooth,' but I say to you, Offer no violent resistance to one who does evil" (Matthew 5:38-39). We recalled his last words to the church in the Garden of Gethsemane. "Put down the sword. Those who live by the sword will die by the sword." We recalled his steadfast nonviolence and resistance to imperial domination, so we determined to go forward in pursuit of peace, come what may. At the heart of our witness was a vision—a vision of peace and nonviolence that we staked our lives on.

My friend Archbishop Desmond Tutu of South Africa said it best. The legendary anti-apartheid leader and Nobel Peace Prize winner said after September 11 that the millions spent on one U.S. fighter bomber sent to bomb Afghanistan could have built thousands of schools in Afghanistan, one of the poorest nations in the world. Instead of bombing Afghanistan in a spirit of retaliatory eye-for-an-eye violence, the United States could have built schools, homes, and hospitals—and in the process, won over the hearts of Muslims everywhere. We already had the sympathy of the world, and if we had responded through the methodology of nonviolence, we could have transformed Afghanistan and the whole world into a new culture of peace. Instead, we resorted to the useless eye-for-an-eye insanity of retaliation. Actually, Afghanistan had nothing to do with September 11: those attacks were funded and planned by Saudi Arabia, one of the worst dictatorships on the planet, where people regularly have their hands and heads chopped off. We used September 11 to invade Afghanistan and later Iraq so we could steal their oil and natural resources, sell billions of dollars in weapons, and begin a new era of permanent warfare.

"Without a vision, the people perish," the book of Proverbs declares. We had lost our vision and become, as Dorothy Day predicted, "the blindest of the blind." The only way forward, the only way out of our insane war making, the only way toward global survival was through Jesus' visionary nonviolence. Jesus was right: we need to put down the sword, reject the way of war and bombing, look into the eyes of sisters and brothers around the world, and pursue nonviolent conflict resolution and God's reign of nonviolence. My friends and I decided that we would deepen our active nonviolence and proclaim it far and wide in order to spread the message and help others discover a new way forward.

We decided that the opposite teaching from the book of Proverbs was also true: "With a vision of peace and nonviolence, the people will live."

It's been a record of setbacks and roadblocks ever since, but a series of breakthroughs and new connections as well. We began to realize in ever-deeper ways the truth of Martin Luther King Jr.'s last words. The night before he was killed, he told the crowd in Memphis, "The choice is no longer violence or nonviolence. It's nonviolence—or nonexistence."

That truth is now playing out before our eyes every day, as our global addiction threatens the earth itself. Our task is to help one another choose wisely.

Violence or nonviolence.

Nonviolence or nonexistence.

Life in all its fullness or death for one and all.

Like people everywhere, we choose nonviolence and the fullness of life. It's the only sane choice.

CHAPTER 2

Journey to the New Mexico Desert

By 2002, my peace work had become too hot to handle for various New York church leaders and I was ordered to leave the city. Long ago, friends in New Mexico said with a laugh, when they finally kick you out of New York, come out here to the desert. I remembered the offer, made a few phone calls, flew out for interviews with church officials, and, before I knew it, was assigned as the pastor of five parishes in the impoverished high desert of northeastern New Mexico.

This was a turning point in my long pilgrimage. I had lived in over forty places and held a variety of positions—from high school teacher to university professor to elementary school principal to community center director to assistant director of a homeless shelter to assistant pastor to assistant to the director of the Robert F. Kennedy Foundation. I had lived in a refugee camp in El Salvador, worked at a human rights center in Belfast, Northern Ireland, and served time in jail in North Carolina for a Plowshares disarmament act of civil disobedience. I was used to feeling rootless, if not downright homeless, but for me, it was always a long pilgrimage of peace, a long journey, a long zigzag life. New Mexico sounded like another adventure in my unexpected, unexplainable, unaccountable peacemaking journey.

I set off with eyes wide open. One of the most beautiful places in North America, New Mexico, is also the poorest. In recent years, it's ranked first in child hunger, poverty, domestic violence, drunk driving, and suicide, and worst in education and health care. But, on the other hand, it's also ranked first in military spending, military recruiting, and development of weapons of mass destruction. New Mexico is the birthplace of the atomic bomb; its first explosion was at Alamogordo, and Los Alamos is the center of all our nuclear weapons development. Yet in the midst of this poverty, starvation, and need, Los Alamos has more millionaires and Ph.D.s per capita than anywhere else on the planet. Here in the peaceful landscape of sagebrush, junipers, coyotes, and red rocks, the blindness of violence breeds nuclear annihilation. Here in the most beautiful place in North America, we plot the end of the world.

I loaded up a U-Haul truck with papers and books, and drove for a week from Broadway in Manhattan to the high desert of northeastern New Mexico. Off Interstate 25, I drove down Main Street in Springer to the large brown church and the old white house next door. Thirty miles down the road, past Ted Turner's ranch, I was given another rectory, next to the parish in the village of Cimarron, a mythical Wild West town of nine hundred where the lone restaurant and hotel still bear the marks of bullet holes from a shootout by Jesse James. Until fifty years ago, the branch hanging over the one and only road through town was from the official hanging tree. The little cemetery high up in the surrounding green hills included the grave of the priest shot dead by his parishioners in the 1880s. Several other churches and missions together kept me busy with six Masses on weekends, countless committee meetings, Confirmation classes, weddings, and funerals regularly for the next few years. I served those parishes with all my energy and strength, presided at a thousand Masses, preaching the good news of peace and love, facilitated scores of funerals, and generally served anyone in need—all while discovering the endless beauty of the New Mexico wilderness. I wasn't on the crowded dirty sidewalks of Broadway anymore.

But the wars continued. The U.S. war in Afghanistan raged on, while a second equally insane war on Iraq began in March

2003. Invitations to speak out against war at rallies, peace conferences, churches, and universities across the nation poured in, so during the week, I often flew off to speak against war and for God's way of peace. A month before the Iraq war began, I was the featured speaker, along with Jesse Jackson and Al Sharpton, at the massive rally in front of the U.S. Capitol in Washington, DC. It was bitter cold, but 300,000 strong cheered my impassioned plea to do everything they could to protest this war, and work for peaceful, nonviolent solutions. I was the lead story on *ABC World News Tonight*, and my antiwar message went out far and wide.

Such talk and public exposure only infuriated the conservative Catholics in one of my mission churches. The entire parish went to the archbishop and asked for my removal. A longtime supporter of war and nuclear weapons, he readily agreed. A few months later, I woke to find the entire National Guard unit of northern New Mexico marching outside the rectory at dawn. They held up their rifles and shouted out the battalion slogan, "One bullet, one kill." I thought for sure they had come to kill me, but I marched outside into their midst, launched into a sermon about Jesus and nonviolence, ordered them to put down their guns, quit the military, and join the global movement for peace. They walked away with their jaws hanging down.

By now the locals—and the entire state it seemed—were quite sick of my antiwar talk and nonstop talk about loving nonviolence. After prayer and discernment with my spiritual director, I stepped down as a local pastor to speak out pastorally for peace to the nation and the world. I had started Pax Christi New Mexico, a branch of the international Catholic peace movement, and a dozen chapters sprang up around the state, with ordinary New Mexicans meeting and praying regularly now for peace. I was thinking of moving back to New York, but some of them urged me to stay in New Mexico, to keep the nascent movement going. On a whim, I agreed. But where to live?

My friend Bud Ryan offered to find me a place. "What are you looking for?" he asked.

"I want a small, simple hermitage on the top of a mountain between Albuquerque and Santa Fe that looks out in every direction over a hundred miles at the vast New Mexico wilderness, that's off the grid, with solar panels, a remote driveway that's impossible to find, and friendly landlords. In other words, a place of perfect peace and quiet, at one with the earth, at the end of the world."

We both laughed. "Well, good luck with that," he said.

That was Tuesday night. The next morning he called and said, "Well, you're not going to believe it, but there's a little house on a mesa just south of Santa Fe that's off the grid and exactly as you described. If you want it, you should leave this minute and I'll arrange for us to meet the landlords at noon."

I hopped into my truck, drove three hours south, and met Bud on the Turquoise Trail, Route 14, at the turnoff of a long dirt road. Leaving my truck by the road, I climbed into his and set off farther into the isolated New Mexico landscape. It was a four-mile drive on rugged dirt paths, filled with ruts and rocks. At the llama farm, we turned left, then drove straight up two steep dirt cliffs until we reached the top of the remote mesa.

Suddenly, we were on top of the world, at the end of the world. The blue sky was so big, it surrounded us, and came at us in all directions, as if we had stepped into it. Along the single-lane dirt road, we passed large green juniper trees, yellow chamisa shrubs, cholla cactus, prickly pear cactus, and unusual brown or gray volcanic-like rocks. In the distance, on every side, mountains traced the horizon.

After several miles on a dirt road with not a house in sight, we came to a grass clearing. I caught my breath. Now we were really in the middle of a 360-degree view. Due north lay Santa Fe at the foot of the Sangre de Cristo mountains leading up into the Rockies, Colorado, and Canada; to the far east, a strange mountain that sloped up to a peak, exactly like Yeats's

Ben Bilbo in the West of Ireland; to the south below us lay the Galisteo basin, beyond that the Ortiz Mountains, and beyond that, the Sandias with Albuquerque on the other side, about seventy-five miles away; and to the west, the Jemez Mountains going up into Los Alamos, the real end of the world, the birthplace of the atomic bomb, hell on earth.

We crawled along an even smaller dirt road, through the juniper and pinon, passed a small, striking two story adobe-ish house, and around a circle to another little brown house with a tin metal roof. Through the front screen door and porch, we walked into a couple of large rooms with bricks on the floor, white walls, and dark brown vigas on the ceiling that look like dark-stained, carved telephone poles holding up the roof. The landlords, Renea and Mat, welcomed me. A year earlier, they had moved out here. They lived in the main house while fixing up the little guesthouse to rent out, with a desire to live in closer rhythm with nature. Their aspiration was to live at one with the earth.

"In the 1970s, some California 'ex-pats' moved to the mesa and together hand built a number of houses, even a schoolhouse, with a community focus," Renea explained. "This guesthouse was made by pouring pumice-crete bucket by bucket into wall forms by a couple in their later years. The vigas were actually ponderosa pines left from a nearby forest fire that were hand peeled by the couple," she said.

We walked out onto the porch and looked out over a hundred miles of junipers, desert, canyons, and distant mountains.

I was overwhelmed. I knew this was a moment of reckoning.

"I'll take it," I said. "When can I move in?"

They smiled, we picked a date, and a month later I moved. And just like that, I became a modern-day desert father, the classic guru on his mountaintop, alone in his solitude to think deep thoughts and center himself in the peace of God.

And what happened? Instead, I became one with earth.

It was not what I expected.

Moving day was April 1, but I was too excited, so I asked Renea and Mat if I could move in a day earlier. I loaded up my books and papers, said goodbye to Springer and Cimarron, and drove south to the Galisteo mesa. My plan was to hit the road, travel the nation and the world, speak out against war and for peace, and write books and essays on the wisdom of nonviolence. The house on the mesa would be my base, but a temporary home, a mountaintop retreat between speaking gigs and tours. It was a world away from Broadway and Manhattan, but also a world away from Santa Fe and Albuquerque. How could I know if I was making the right decision? I couldn't. I could only follow my heart, pray for guidance, and carry on the journey.

It was March 31, a Tuesday afternoon, when I pulled up to the ramshackle "adobe" home. Just at that moment, after a long, cold winter, spring arrived. The temperature soared into the 60s. A gentle rain began to fall upon the desert. There is nothing to compare with the freshness of the desert after a rain. Steam rises from the sand. Everything is clean. I walked into the house alone. There was nothing there—no furniture, no decorations, no lights, no drinking water, no food. But the fresh air from the desert rain lifted a fresh fragrance into the house. The sun began to set in the West. Its strong rays beamed throughout the house like spotlights, while outside the sky turned a psychedelic blue, green, orange, red, and yellow. I threw open the doors and windows and let the fresh spring air fill the house. It was Easter, and I felt in my bones a new beginning, a new day, a new spirit of peace, as if I was at the dawn of creation, stepping into the Garden of Eden, coming into the light after forty days on a rain-drenched ark.

I sat on the red brick floor in the middle of the big room that functioned as kitchen, dining room, and living room combined, with white walls and brown wood beams overhead and tried to take it all in. It was perfect—perfect silence, perfect solitude, perfect peace. I had never experienced such silence, such solitude, such peace before. The silence was otherworldly—not a car, not a sound, nothing. I was overwhelmed with a sense of consolation.

Just then, all of a sudden, a large white bird flew into the room through the open back screen door. It was a massive white dove, unlike anything I had seen before. It was fast, and white, and full of energy. It flew over me and then around the room for twenty minutes, in circles, its wings flapping nonstop. I was terrified. I didn't know what to do, or how to get it outside. I stood up, I ducked, I sat down, and I let it fly around me.

Minutes went by. It kept flying over me. I was electrified, terrified, and exhilarated; so was the dove! Then, after twenty minutes, as quickly as it appeared, it flew directly out the back door and disappeared into the desert horizon and the glorious sunset. Just as suddenly, I was back alone in my barren room.

I immediately thought of the dove that appeared to Noah on the ark. Then I remembered the dove that hovered over Jesus as he emerged from the Jordan River, just after his baptism. In that moment, Noah found hope for a future of peace with creation. In that moment, Jesus discovered his calling, to be who he was, the beloved son of God, a peacemaker, sent on a mission of peace to lead humanity and all creation into God's realm of perfect peace.

"God must want me to stay here," I thought to myself. "This is a good sign. God is anointing me for something. God is blessing me."

I threw down some blue-and-white horse blankets on the floor and covered myself with blue-and-white Mexican blankets. In the pitch-black night, I tried to sleep, but was shaking with excitement. "The Spirit of the Lord," to quote Isaiah and Luke, "was upon me."

A new journey was beginning. I was stepping into the peace of creation itself.

CHAPTER 3

The Vision of a New Heaven and a New Earth

That little adobe shack on the mesa turned out to be more just than a dwelling. It is a house of peace, a sanctuary of peace, a hermitage of peace, unlike anything I have experienced or seen before. This is the kind of dwelling Thomas Merton came to New Mexico in search of in May 1968, just months before his untimely death. For someone who has spent his life speaking and advocating for peace, it is an undeserved blessing, a revelation, a calling.

Today, if you sought out that house, you'd have to travel long and hard, and still you'd never find it. No one can. There's no address, no road, no mailbox, no street, no nothing. It's the middle of nowhere, at the end of the earth, on top of the world. But if you have a third eye, it's at the center of creation.

A few small, odd-looking houses lie hidden around the mesa, if you look carefully, but for all intents and purposes, I am alone. But not quite alone. A pair of giant white jack rabbits live nearby. Brown coyotes wander around the house each night. Little white rabbits surround the deck each morning at sunrise. Spectacular green and blue hummingbirds pay a visit each summer morning. Then there's the occasional rattlesnake, tarantula, scorpion, or centipede—and even more impressively, the mountain lion that shows up every few years, not to mention the massive black ravens that swoop down from behind with their four-foot wingspan leaving a strong wind in their wake and their loud cries hanging in the air. In the summer, the nighthawks dive down through the air at sunset, emitting a strange sound like the muted roar of a mountain lion. It's a whole new world, a world beyond my imagining, the real world, far from the illusions of the big city.

Once, as I stood by the back window talking on the phone with my dear friend and teacher, Father Daniel Berrigan, a brown coyote walked right up to the window, looking right at me. "Dan, I'm living the movie *Dances with Wolves*," I said. Not long ago, another coyote walked right up to me, looking at me through the back window. Then her four coyote pups stepped from behind the juniper and stood there looking at me for thirty seconds. In that same spot, a few weeks later, while friends were gathered around my table for a fine meal, a bobcat walked up to the window, stopped in its tracks, looked at us. We were overwhelmed. After taking our measure, it walked on by.

From outside, it's just a small brown, adobe-looking house with a tin roof and big windows painted bright blue. In Santa Fe, many brown adobe homes have blue doors and blue windows. The colors match the brown desert floor and the infinite blue sky. But when you step into the poor little house, it becomes a large, expansive place of peace. The little front porch has an old handmade wooden bench painted bright blue. Its walls are white, and a beautiful blue handmade rectangular pottery sign hangs near the dark wooden door with the greeting "Peace be with you."

The first room is long. You look up and see rows of large, dark, hand-carved, smooth wooden beams that stretch across the ceiling. The floor is made of dark, smooth wooden boards. On either side the walls have tall brown bookcases filled with books, artwork, photos, awards, and knickknacks from my world travels. At the end stands a massive kiva-like fireplace that has a circular mantle covered with icons and little statues of Jesus and the saints. On one wall is a large print of color-ful life in Mexico given to me by my friend, musician Carlos Santana. Two large wooden chairs sit before a large window that looks out at a distant mountain range, where on one of the peaks, Los Alamos, birthplace of the atomic bomb, stands like Mordor. It's paradise, but it's also *Lord of the Rings*.

You step left into the large main room. This time the floor is made of red brick, and the white walls are covered with art-work and photos of heroes and friends. On one side, over my desk, hang pictures of Gandhi, Oscar Romero, Merton, and Nelson Mandela, along with my friends Daniel Berrigan, Joan Baez, Jackson Browne, Helen Prejean, Mairead Maguire, and Martin Sheen. By the door next to the little porch, a beautiful, large color photo of Dr. King hangs on the wall, along with original artwork by Corita Kent for the Plowshares Eight, with the words "We Are Filled with Hope." Above that hangs orig-inal handmade calligraphy by the Buddhist Zen master Thich Nhat Hanh that reads "Peace Is Every Step." Next to it, the large woodcut of Jesus breaking a rifle on his knee, made by a German peace activist/artist during the Nazi era.

Overhead, long wooden beams stretch across the ceiling. A large blue couch sits in the center and in front of it a mas-sive, low, dark wooden table, which was actually the door of a ship that crashed on the Outer Banks of North Carolina in the 1800s, near the place where I was born. A whole wall of windows opens the room onto the vast panorama—my own private Grand Canyon, an infinitely interesting vista of juni-pers and yellow chamisa shrubs, arroyos, and cliffs, and distant valleys and canyons. A few mornings each year, I rise and look out past the edge of the mesa to see down below a layer of puffy white clouds, and I realize that I dwell above the clouds, in the heavens.

I am way off the grid, with no landline phone, no utility-based electricity, and no drinking water. A kitchen sink and cabinets and counter line the far side of the room, all painted blue by me. An old propane refrigerator stands at the end, covered with a hundred beautiful postcards. This room is my home. When I sit on the couch and look out at the horizon surrounded by this cloud of witnesses, I feel like I'm on a spaceship, ready for liftoff. On second thought, I've never felt so grounded.

The little bathroom off to the side is painted bright blue, yellow, and white. The walls are covered with fifty framed awards, posters, and fliers announcing various speaking events and retreats around the world. The bedroom is another long, white-walled room with dark wood beams across the ceiling, several large glass windows, and original icons hanging on the walls.

In the storage area just before the bathroom lie the large batteries for the simple solar panels lined up outside along the edge of the house. I was so excited when I first moved off the grid, to rely solely on the sun for my electricity. But it took some getting used to. In December, the sun goes down fast. Some days can be entirely dark. If you are not careful, you can run out of your entire electrical supply within five days. If it's a harsh winter, the darkness can last for months. In that case, you learn not to use electricity, except only what's needed. You keep your lights off, unplug everything, and don't even use the coffee maker, which takes up a surprisingly large amount of current. You make coffee by boiling water. You make toast by placing it on a pan over the stove. You read by sunlight, go to bed early, and get up early. Fifteen years later, this rhythm is perfectly natural. I'm used to living according to the rhythm of the sun and the moon, and I enjoy it. I feel more at home, part of the ecological balance. Now, when I go to bed on a wintry night and hear the howling of the coyotes out in the snow, under the shining moon, I feel at peace, one with the circle of life.

I live here alone, except for a black-and-white tuxedo cat named "Cimarron," after my old parish. She is gentle and loving, but moody and independent. She was a Zen Buddhist nun in a previous lifetime, I've decided. I know this because when I sit for morning meditation, she sits in the big, white, broad windowsill with her back very straight and her head slightly bent down. She doesn't move for an hour, but practices perfect mindfulness, concentrating on her in-breath, letting her mind settle down. She might also just be sleeping. The mere smell of her presence keeps the desert creatures outside, but occasionally, in the middle of the night, she wakes me up by standing on my chest and dropping a dead mouse on me as a gift of love. Sometimes the mice are still alive, and I have to try to capture them and release them outside into the desert before she catches them again. Even the house of peace has its moments of war.

Over the years, Mat and Renea have come over occasionally for dinner, or have me over to their house. We keep an eye on each other, as well as the handful of other neighbors, many of whom work in the movie industry. Once, a tornado touched down about a mile away. I was away, and Renea was ready to rescue the cat and drive off the mesa, but it evaporated as fast as it appeared. On another day, a fire started a mile away, but the local volunteer fire department put it out quickly. Then, while I was away in Ireland, rumors spread of a mountain lion that was stalking the mesa for a few weeks. After I returned, one Sunday morning, I saw him walk by. I was so shaken, I called the New Mexico game warden, who was unimpressed and not interested. "If he attacks you or your dog, call me back," he said before hanging up. Here was a lesson for life in the desert. One particular summer, we were inundated with ten-foot-long green-and-gold rattlesnakes. If they bite you, you can be dead within fifteen minutes. We wouldn't make it off the mesa. So we avoid them, and they avoid us, and everyone survives as we go about our business.

One year it never rained. Then after this long drought, one Friday the clouds turned black and it rained six inches in two hours. The dirt roads were flooded and turned into a sea of mud. No one could drive up the mesa for weeks. Several houses were flooded from the leaky ceilings. Parts of my house were soaked.

On another day in July, I noticed the sun disappear, the sky turn black, and the temperature plummet to freezing. Then, out of nowhere, a ferocious hailstorm broke out. My tin roof was pounded, and I thought the whole ceiling was going to fall in. Large white hailstones fell across the desert floor, turning the desert white before my eyes, as if it had a new layer of snow. An hour later, the sun reappeared, the sky turned blue, the temperature rose, and the hail vanished. I would not have believed it if I hadn't seen it with my own eyes.

At night, thousands of stars turn out, sometimes it seems like a million. Usually, a wide stretch of pink cloud crosses the night sky, the Milky Way. One night every August, thousands of shooting stars cross the New Mexico sky in a spectacular show of beauty. One year, my friend Fr. Patrick was visiting from the West of Ireland, so we set up lounge chairs on the back porch at 11 p.m. and poured ourselves some wine and watched the evening show. It was beautiful, until all of a sudden, a large ball of fire the size of the moon shot across the sky and fell into the distant mountains. We both jumped up instinctively and started screaming, thinking the end of the world had come. In the morning paper, we read that it was just a meteor, the size of a penny, that made such a spectacle.

The most difficult experience I had occurred shortly after Christmas during my first or second year. It was a dark, quiet day, at the end of December, and it started to snow and snow and snow. It didn't stop snowing for three full days. By the end, three feet of snow covered the mesa. The drifts around my house were five feet high. There was nowhere to go. The car was buried. The junipers disappeared under the blanket of snow. I had no electricity, no TV, no phone, no radio, no computer, but I did have heat, and the old stove worked fine.

I made big fires and sat before the fireplace to keep warm. I cooked soup, made sandwiches, and drank a little wine. I read and prayed and looked out the window and studied my book shelves. For eight long days, I was stranded, like everyone else on the mesa. I felt like Robert Redford in the movie *Jeremiah Johnson*, living alone in the wintry wild. Relief came when a massive plow, sent by the city, made its way along our dirt roads, up our steep hill, and right up to our front doors. It was a powerful test of winter solitude, and while it was peaceful and beautiful, I'm not sure I want to do that again.

In other words, you never know what to expect living off the grid, alone in the high desert. The elements, the creatures, the environment, it turns out, are in charge. You are not.

Just the other day, after I returned from a trip to California, Renea told me about her daily visits to the house to feed the cat. We were mesmerized by a pair of birds that had set up their nest every year in the wooden beams hanging over my deck, but last year, moved to the radar dish for my Internet service. It's a thick, stainless steel, four-foot-tall round pole that rises to a metal plate where the radar disk sits. For the second year in a row, the birds showed up, but this time, they built a beautiful nest overnight right there on the metal plate, just below the radar disk. For three weeks, the mother bird sat on her eggs, some days in one-hundred-degree heat. We were so moved. While I was away, Renea placed a bowl of water for her nearby. Then, in time, four eggs hatched, and four little birdlings stuck their heads up crying out for food. It was magical.

Renea was telling me about the birds on my return, when she made a passing comment. "I'm really trying to be fully present to nature from now on. Nature is such a great teacher. I want to see nature with my eyes wide open, to take it all in, to really notice what's happening right now in the moment and to remain as peaceful, present, and centered as possible."

There lies a path for all of us. The old ways are over. From now on, we all have to open our eyes, look at nature and be fully present and take it all in. That marks a new path for a future of peace, but it requires vision. We have to wake up and open our eyes to creation.

From Broadway to Cimarron to the mesa overlooking the Galisteo basin, from the yelling, screaming, and sirens of the Upper West Side to the desolate mountaintop where the silence is overwhelming unless the coyotes start howling, I've undergone a journey toward solidarity with Mother Earth and her creatures. My new life on the mesa, on Mother Earth, amazes me with slow, peaceful daily revelations that awaken my heart and give me hope. My trips and speaking events continue, but I always return home to the mesa. I've traveled throughout Australia, New Zealand, England, Scotland, Ireland, Italy, Germany, Mexico, and Canada, speaking for peace. Every few years, I embark on a long book tour, traveling to nearly all fifty states to speak about my latest work. Sometimes I head off to a demonstration, and sometimes I land in jail, but eventually I make it back to the mesa. And every August, friends from across the state and I travel up the mountain road to Los Alamos in August, on the anniversary of the U.S. atomic bombing of Hiroshima, to pray, speak out, and protest the ongoing, insane development of nuclear weapons.

Are we a threat to the national laboratories? Are we a threat to national security? Of course not. We are ordinary citizens, church folk, public peacemakers, but our witness attracts front-page attention and widespread attack. Maybe that's because we don't shout or scream. We sit down in ashes, put on sackcloth, and pray in repentance.

Yes, that's right, we sit in sackcloth and ashes. What could be more ridiculous? And yet, I submit, everyone in Los Alamos, and in New Mexico, knows exactly what we are doing, what we are saying. The God of peace considers the development of nuclear weapons to be the ultimate mortal sin, the ultimate blasphemy. We repent publicly for that mortal sin, without pointing judgmental fingers at anyone. We try to embody the spirit of nonviolence we call for, the spirit of peace we feel in the beauty of creation around us, the vision of a nuclear-free, nonviolent world to come. And we take a stand on behalf of the world's poor, Mother Earth and her creatures, that we might all survive in peace.

It's not rocket science. It's simply the wisdom and way of nonviolence. We are called to be nonviolent to ourselves, nonviolent to one another, nonviolent to the creatures and to Mother Earth, which means we spend our lives on a new journey, a gospel journey, living a countercultural life in peace, hope, and love. We will probably be ignored and make no difference, but we will try and do our best to welcome a new world of nonviolence.

The nonviolent Jesus taught this long ago. He mapped out the way forward when no one even knew there was an alternative. So we turn to him and his road map for clues about a future of peace with creation and one another.

CHAPTER 4

Walking on Earth Like the Nonviolent Jesus

I step out the front screen door and follow the dirt path around to the triangle at the center of the mesa. This is my favorite walk. Standing there you have a 360-degree view, with the big sky bearing down upon you. Santa Fe and the Rockies are due north; Los Alamos and the Jemez Mountains due west; the plains going east; and the Sandia Mountains and Albuquerque due south. At eight thousand feet high, it's my own mountain-top panorama. Then, I follow the dirt path over a mile to the hill. It's the only road to my house and the other houses on the mesa, so I know it like the back of my hand. That helps, because I'm a daydreamer, and the minute I step off the path, I would get lost in the desert. It's no joke. Within five minutes, you can be completely lost, with no bearings about your surroundings. Everything looks the same, so you can be dangerously stuck.

So I stay on the path and walk to the hill, where I stop and catch my breath and look out over miles of spectacular scenery. It reminds me so much of the landscape I saw during my travels through India, and I love it. I feel so blessed to be here, to walk this earth, to practice peace on this path, to let my spirit soar, my heart widen, and my mind turn back to the nonviolent Jesus, the only one I'm interested in following.

The nonviolent Jesus shows us how to live in right relationship with Mother Earth and her creatures. If Gandhi was right—that Jesus was the embodiment of nonviolence—then Jesus' nonviolence extends to everyone and everything, including every creature and Mother Earth herself. If we take the time to study his life, we find clues about how to live in peace on earth amid these creatures with every other human being, even in a time of catastrophic climate change. As his disciples, we need to regroup, recommit ourselves to following him, and do as he does, even if we do not understand him or know where he is going. We need to place our trust in Jesus, trusting especially that all answers can be found in our discipleship to him, in walking the earth in his gentle footsteps on that humble path of nonviolence.

The four Gospels portray Jesus as a pilgrim of peace walking from Galilee to Jerusalem, where he eventually confronted the imperial system head-on and gave his life for humanity and the coming of God's reign of peace and nonviolence. With every step, he noticed everything, everyone, and every landscape. He never went far from home. Raised in Galilee, in an impoverished desert region, he walked from town to town, often slept outdoors, never settled down, and eventually made his way to Jerusalem. His geography was a mere ninety miles at best, but he knew the landscape, and with it, the people and the creatures.

Jesus could talk about birds, fish, chickens, sheep, lambs, fig trees, cedars, wheat fields, corn, and vineyards. He knew every path, every hill and mountain, river and sea. He could discuss the weather, the sky, the feel of the air. He was one with his environment. He was fully present to everyone, every creature, every inch of land, and everywhere around him, he saw the finger of God. His vision of life and the way he lived on that small patch of earth model the way we too can relate to the earth and her creatures, as well as to one another.

During his pilgrimage on earth, he modeled the fullest human life of loving nonviolence. Because he was nonviolent to the core of his being, he was one with God and all humanity. But he was also one with Mother Earth and her creatures, with all creation. He knew and loved the earth and its creatures. He was at peace with one and all, even as he tried to stop the violence around him.

Jesus respected Mother Earth and pondered her mysteries as indigenous peoples have always done—to find hidden clues about the will of God. His peaceful, respectful, loving attitude toward the earth, her creatures, and all human beings sets the norm for human life and the way out of our madness. If we are to survive, we need to return to that same kind of nonviolent living and respect for one another, the earth, and all her creatures. In Jesus, we find our way out, our way forward, our way to peace.

"The Lord was able to invite others to be attentive to the beauty that there is in the world because he himself was in constant touch with nature, lending it an attention full of fondness and wonder," Pope Francis writes. "As he made his way throughout the land, he often stopped to contemplate the beauty sown by his Father, and invited his disciples to perceive a divine message in things: 'Lift up your eyes, and see how the fields are ready for harvest' (Jn 4:35). 'The kingdom of God is like a grain of mustard seed which a man took and sowed in his field; it is the smallest of all seeds, but once it has grown, it is the greatest of plants' (Mt 13:31-32)."[1]

Jesus was a great walker. He walked everywhere. He knew the earth well because he spent his life walking on it. The Gospels teach that he was baptized in the Jordan River, and then, as he prayed by the river, a dove hovered over him and he realized his vocation to be the beloved son of God. Then he walked into the wilderness where he fasted and prayed for forty days, "among the wild beasts," we're told. Then he set off on his walking campaign, going from village to village with his community of disciples around him—healing the sick, teaching nonviolence, expelling the demons of violence and proclaiming the coming of God's reign of peace and nonviolence. He climbed mountains, slept outdoors, rode the waters, noticed animals and children, and lived simply and totally in the present moment of peace.

Like the Buddha, every step for Jesus was made in peace and mindfulness. Wherever he went, he left an imprint of peace. He embodied the connection between nonviolence and care for the earth. In other words, he could announce the beatitude of meekness and nonviolence, and their connection with the earth, because he first lived it to the full. He expects his followers to try to do the same, come what may.

Jesus' Life of Nonviolence

Jesus' life is the story of nonviolence. By the Jordan River, Jesus learns that God is a God of nonviolent love and that he is the beloved son of God. In the desert, he is tempted to reject that identity and choose the way of violence. Instead, he renounces the temptations of violence, including the temptation to become the violent messiah that many Jews under Roman occupation were expecting. He claims his identity as the nonviolent, beloved son of the God of peace. He goes forth into the culture of war and empire as a peacemaker, as the embodiment of nonviolence, and invites everyone to share in this life of peace and nonviolence.

In the Sermon on the Mount, Jesus teaches a broad vision of nonviolence. He invites everyone to become a peacemaker, and thus, to become who they were created to be—like him, the sons and daughters of the God of peace. "Blessed are the peacemakers; they shall be called the sons and daughters of the God of peace," he declares. "Offer no violent resistance to one who does evil. When someone strikes you on the right cheek, turn the other cheek. Love your enemies and pray for your persecutors, that you may be sons and daughters of your heavenly God who lets his sun rise on the good and the bad and the rain to fall on the just and the unjust. Do unto others as you would have them do unto you. Forgive and you will be forgiven. Be as compassionate as God. Seek first God's kingdom and God's justice and everything will be provided for you."

As he teaches nonviolence, Jesus also practices and embodies nonviolence. He heals the sick and disabled, the victims of the culture of violence; he expels the demons of violence, in particular, our possessions and allegiance to empire and the culture of war; and he welcomes God's reign of nonviolence by proclaiming it and making it real—by feeding the hungry and liberating the oppressed. His nonviolent resistance to violence confronts systemic dehumanization, such as when he defies the sabbath laws to heal the man with the withered hand (Mark 3:1-6) or when he peacefully but determinedly challenges the religious men who accuse a woman of adultery and threaten to kill her (John 8:1-11). He literally stops the killing and saves her life. His new commandment outlaws violence once and for all: "Let the one without sin be the first to throw a stone at her."

There are innumerable examples of his active nonviolence throughout the four Gospels. He is never passive or weak. His proactive nonviolence is the power of love and truth in action. Halfway through Luke's account, Jesus organizes his followers in peace teams and sends them on a mission of nonviolence into the culture of violence. He does this first with his twelve apostles, and then again with seventy-two disciples. "I am sending you out as lambs sent into the midst of wolves," he declares, making it clear that they are to be as harmless and nonviolent as lambs. Everywhere they go, they are to be peaceful, to speak words of peace, and to offer the blessings of peace.

Like him, they are to heal people who have been victims of the culture of violence; expel the demons of violence, war, and empire so that people can live in the freedom of peace and nonviolence; and proclaim the coming of God's kingdom of nonviolence, a whole new world without war, poverty, oppression, empire, and systemic injustice. The seventy-two set out, fulfill the mission, and come back rejoicing. Wow, this really works! they say to Jesus. In response, we're told, Jesus starts rejoicing, too. One could argue that it is the only time in the four Gospels when Jesus experiences joy—because his followers did what he said and undertook and completed his public mission of creative nonviolence.

Jesus can send his disciples on a campaign of nonviolence because he himself lived a lifelong campaign of nonviolence. At some point along his walking journey, we're told, he set his face to Jerusalem, like Gandhi on the Salt March, and walked toward it. As he approached it, he broke down weeping, saying, "If this day you had only known the things that make for peace!" Then he engaged in nonviolent direct action to confront the empire's systemic injustice. He was arrested, tortured, and executed, and remained peaceful and nonviolent until his last breath.

Learning with Jesus from Mother Earth and Her Creatures

Many of Jesus' teachings are rooted in nature. In the Sermon on the Mount, he calls people to be "the salt of the earth" (Matt. 5:13). He suggests that human beings give flavor to creation, that we are here to improve creation for the Creator, not destroy it. When he describes God's inherent nature of unconditional, universal love, he looks to creation for evidence. God, he announces, "makes his sun rise on the bad and the good and causes rain to fall on the just and the unjust" (Matt. 5:45). When asked how we should pray, he instructs us to pray that heaven come down to earth. "This is how you are to pray: Our Father in heaven, hallowed be your name, your kingdom come, your will be done, on earth as in heaven" (Matt. 6:9-10). In each case, he describes godly living and human living based on the evidence of Mother Earth and her creatures.

Learn to depend entirely on God, he teaches, and do so by studying creation. "Look at the birds in the sky; they do not sow or reap; they gather nothing into barns, yet your heavenly Father feeds them. Are not you more important than they?" he asks. "Learn from the way the wildflowers grow. They do not work or spin. But I tell you that not even Solomon in all his splendor was clothed like one of them. If God so clothes the grass of the field, which grows today and is thrown into the oven tomorrow, will God not much more provide for you? . . . Seek first the kingdom of God and God's justice and all these things will be given you besides" (Matt. 6:25-34).

"We read in the Gospel that Jesus says of the birds of the air that 'not one of them is forgotten before God' (Lk. 12:6)," Pope Francis comments. "How then can we possibly mistreat them or cause them harm? I ask all Christians to recognize and to live fully this dimension of their conversion. May the power and the light of the grace we have received also be evident in our relationship to other creatures and to the world around us. In this way, we will help nurture that sublime fraternity with all creation which Saint Francis of Assisi so radiantly embodied."[2]

"Every good tree bears good fruit, and a rotten tree bears bad fruit," Jesus concludes in the Sermon on the Mount. Bear good fruit for God with your lives, he teaches. "By their fruits you will know them" (Matt. 5:17, 20). "Either declare the tree good and its fruit is good or declare the tree rotten and its fruit is rotten, for a tree is known by its fruit. . . . A good person brings forth good out of a store of goodness, but an evil person brings forth evil out of a store of evil" (Matt. 12:33-35). With his study of trees and fruits, he explains to us the meaning of life.

In the conclusion of the Sermon on the Mount, he tells a parable about a terrible storm destroying the house where we live. If we have built our house solidly on rock, we will withstand the storm. If not, our house will be destroyed (Matt. 5:24-27). That, he teaches, is the way of life. At some point, you will be hit by a storm. Only those who follow his teachings on love, peace, compassion, and nonviolence in the Sermon on the Mount, who build their lives on these solid foundations, will survive the catastrophic storm to come.

Describing his own life, he compared himself to animals: "Foxes have dens and birds of the sky have nests, but the Son of Humanity has nowhere to rest his head" (Matt. 6:20). He even likens himself to a mother hen who gathers her chicks under her wings. He compares his work to the harvest: "The harvest is abundant but the laborers are few, so ask the master of the harvest to send out laborers for his harvest" (Matt. 6:37–38). He sends his disciples out on a mission as laborers sent out for the harvest, and compares them to animals: "I am sending you like sheep in the midst of wolves; be shrewd as serpents and simple as doves" (Matt. 7:16). When persecutions come, he tells us not to be afraid or lose faith in God, who watches over us, just as God watches over creation: "Are not two sparrows sold for a small coin? Yet not one of them falls to the ground without your Father's knowledge. . . . Do not be afraid; you are worth more than many sparrows" (Matt. 10:29).

Throughout the Synoptic Gospels, Jesus speaks in parables to explain life, the kingdom of God, and what we should do. In his parable of the sower, he describes his work and our response. The sower sows good seed. Some falls on the path and the birds eat it; some falls on rocky ground and eventually dies; some falls among thorns, which choke it; and some falls on rich soil, which produce good fruit. He uses a common nature experience to describe how we should receive the word of God, take it to heart, and let it bear good fruit in our lives. In a parable about the kingdom of God, he describes a man who sows good seed in his field, but, then, an enemy comes at night and sows weeds in the field. The owner allows them both to grow until harvest time, when he gathers the wheat for himself and burns the weeds (Matt. 13:24–30). In the parable of the mustard seed, Jesus likens the kingdom of God to a mustard seed, the smallest of all seeds, which becomes a large bush that attracts the birds of the sky, who come to dwell in its branches (Matt. 13:31–32). The birds are a metaphor for all those who live in the kingdom of God. Other images for the kingdom include treasure buried in a field, a pearl of great price, and a dragnet thrown into the sea that collects every kind of fish and object. Over and over he speaks of godly things in terms of earthly things.

A frequent image for the kingdom of God and God's creation is the vineyard. In one parable, he speaks of a landowner who leases his vineyard to tenants and then goes on a long trip. The greedy tenants want the vineyard and its money for themselves, so they punish the servants, torture them, and then, when the owner's son arrives, kill him. What will the owner of the vineyard do to those tenants when he returns? Jesus asks (Matt. 21:33-40). For Jesus, we are merely stewards of Mother Earth, nonviolent people living in and tending the Creator's glorious vineyard. We are not to destroy it or one another, but live and work in peace in this glorious creation. It's time we learn the lesson, Jesus tells us, and do our part to care for the vineyard of creation.

Jesus goes on to describe his presence on earth as "lightning coming from the east and [that] is seen as far as the west" (Matt. 24:27). In other words, his presence, his life, his death, and his resurrection make up the light that lights up creation. But he also describes, in typical apocalyptic tradition, the violent days to come. In light of our rejection of nonviolence, our hatred of one another and the earth, it would make sense that a reasonable person like Jesus discerns the worst to come. After those days he says, "The sun will be darkened, and the moon will not give its light, and the stars will fall from the sky, and the powers of the heavens will be shaken," and then "the sign of the Son of Humanity will appear in heaven . . ." (Matt. 24:29-30). Jesus warns that if we disobey the Creator and reject his teachings of nonviolence, our self-destructive violence will inevitably lead to global destruction.

It's right there in the Gospels. If we continue with our systemic violence, kill one another and destroy creation, if we reject the wisdom and life of creative nonviolence, then our violence will lash back upon us, and we will destroy ourselves and Mother Earth. There are social, economic, political, environmental, and spiritual consequences to our self-destructive violence. We deny his teachings at our own risk. "Those times will have tribulation such has not been since the beginning of God's creation until now, nor ever will be," he says (Mark 13:19).

After these apocalyptic end-time images, he points us once again back to nature: "Learn a lesson from the fig tree. When its branch becomes tender and sprouts leaves, you know that summer is near. In the same way, when you see all these things, know that he is near, at the gates" (Matt. 24:32-33). He's talking about himself, and his peaceful presence. To learn a lesson from a fig tree, we have to be people of contemplative non-violence and mindfulness, who keep watch upon nature, who feel the presence of the God of peace. As we do, we enter into the kingdom of God, the resurrection of peace, and we find a way out of our madness. It is consoling to hear his promise that "he is near." Whatever lies ahead, we know that through our contemplative peace, our oneness with creation and humanity, "he is near." That is a Gospel promise.

Jesus in Bad Weather

Two nature stories stand out as we reflect on Jesus and catastrophic climate change: when Jesus calms a storm at sea, and when he walks on water and calls Peter to walk out on the water with him. Together, they offer a way to face our predicament.

In Matthew's account (Matt. 8:23-27), Jesus and the disciples are out on the Sea of Galilee in a boat, when a violent storm breaks out and fills the boat with water. The disciples are terrified. They think they are about to die. But Jesus sleeps soundly on a cushion. He is unaware of the chaos around him. This dramatic moment contrasts with the later scene in the Garden of Gethsemane, where Jesus prays in panic and agony, hours before his execution, while his beloved disciples sleep soundly around him.

The disciples cry out, "Lord, save us! We are perishing!" Jesus wakes up, rebukes the wind and the sea, and a great calm comes upon the waters. "Why are you terrified, O you of little faith?" he asks them pointedly.

That's the question he asks each one of us today.

In Mark's version (Mark 4:35-40) and Luke's version (Luke 8:22-25), Jesus tells his hapless disciples as they approach the boat, "Let us cross to the other side." It's an important, albeit obvious, detail. The point of the parable is that Jesus is leading the disciples across the great Sea of Galilee to "the other side"—to enemy territory. He's just instructed them to "love your enemies," and now he sends them off into enemy territory to practice what he has preached, this strange new way of universal nonviolent love.

For the disciples, such nonviolent love was terrifying. It continues to terrify and confuse us today. It would be like setting off for Afghanistan, or Iraq, or Syria, or Iran. People would think you're crazy, as I discovered on my journeys to Afghanistan and Iraq. "Why would you go and do a fool thing like that?" many people asked me. For Jesus, loving one's enemies through active, creative nonviolence is the new normal. It's no big deal. Practicing creative nonviolence is easy. In fact, for him, it offers a chance to catch up on some much needed sleep. Finally, he can collapse on a nice soft cushion in the front of a boat out as they set out to sea.

Loving our enemies and practicing loving nonviolence is still like a terrifying boat ride across a turbulent sea. Like the disciples, the mere thought of such a possibility for our own ordinary lives instills anxiety, fear, and terror. Yet despite our fears and concerns, we are summoned to practice the universal love as Jesus, to be as calm and nonviolent as Jesus, to be as trusting as Jesus, and to be as one with creation as Jesus. That is the way forward, the way to peace, the way toward a good sleep out on the sea—by loving our enemies, engaging in active global nonviolence. It is a way to calm even the stormiest sea.

On another occasion, we're told how Jesus sends his disciples off on the boat to the other side while he himself heads up a mountain to spend a night in prayerful communion with God. There out at sea, a storm stirs up, the waves rise up, the boat is tossed about, and once again, the disciples are terrified. The end has come, they think. All is lost. Just then, we're told, "he came toward them, walking on the sea" (Matt. 14:25-33). When the disciples saw Jesus walking on the sea, "they were terrified." "It is a ghost," they said, and they all cried out in fear.

"Take courage, it is I," Jesus said to them. "Do not be afraid."

Here they are, out at sea in a horrific storm, about to die, when Jesus comes walking calmly on the water toward them. This is a moment worth pondering, a scenario that could apply to the whole human race as we face the consequences of our violence in catastrophic climate change.

I think we are in the same boat today. We face the literal storms of catastrophic climate change, we give in to fear and terror and hopelessness, and just then, Jesus comes toward us, walking on the sea, peaceful and calm, right through the storm.

"Lord, if it is you," Peter calls out, according to Matthew's account, "command me to come to you on the water." "Come," Jesus responds. With that, Peter steps out on the water and begins to walk on the water toward Jesus. But as he hears the strong wind and realizes what he is doing, he becomes terrified again and starts to sink. The moment he takes his eyes off Jesus, he sinks. Just about to drown, he cries out to Jesus, who stretches out his hand and catches him. Then he asks Peter with a smile, "O you of little faith, why did you doubt?" Once back in the boat, the storm calms down and they fall at his feet in worship.

Here is a way forward in a time of catastrophic climate change, permanent war, systemic injustice, and the destruction of Mother Earth and her creatures. All we have to do is trust the nonviolent Jesus, live according to his teachings, let go of our fears, place our hope and faith in him, and do what he says. Let me repeat that, even if it sounds like I'm harping: we actually have to do what he says! Even if that means walking out on the stormy waters with him. He is not afraid. We need not be afraid either. There is a way forward, and he knows it and has shared it with us. All we have to do is keep our eyes on him and follow him on his Sermon on the Mount plan of universal nonviolent love.

Like St. Peter, we too can walk on water. Our creative nonviolence can be as easy, as pure, as thorough, and as deep as Jesus. We can cultivate the same fearlessness and faith as he does. If we trust him, look at him, and walk toward him, if we live at one with Mother Earth and all creation, we know that one day the storm will calm down, the sea will calm down, we will calm down, and together we will reach the other side to make peace with our sisters and brothers and welcome God's reign of nonviolence on Mother Earth.

Jesus teaches us how to walk peacefully on earth and treat Mother Earth and her creatures nonviolently. He walked peacefully on earth, and we his followers can do the same. In the process, we will do our part to protect Mother Earth and her creatures and reverse the violence of human-made climate change. From his example, we can learn to live in peace together and protect this beautiful Garden of Eden given to us by the Creator. As we deepen and connect our living nonviolence with our living care for the earth, we can stop the destruction of the earth and her creatures, and work for a more nonviolent world where everyone has adequate food, water, housing, health care, education, employment, and dignity, where it is easier for everyone to live like Jesus in God's kingdom, where even the land and its creatures shine with the fullness of peace.

This is doable. This is what Jesus wants. This is what Jesus showed us to do while he walked Mother Earth. The time has come for us to live just like him and start walking in peace on Mother Earth just like him. That means, of course, some things are going to have to change.

CHAPTER 5

Yosemite and Catastrophic Climate Change

It's another majestic day here in Yosemite National Park in northern California. I've been coming here regularly to preside at Masses for the locals and the tourists at the little mission church, "Our Lady of the Snows," living in one of the dark wooden cabins, right off Yosemite Village, which was given to the local diocese to house visiting priests. This year, I've returned three times for two- to three-week visits. It's a whole new reality amid the redwoods, ponderosas, and sequoias, walking in the glacially sculpted valley, staring up at the towering cliffs and stunning waterfalls, studying the chickaree squirrels and deer as they pass by, and taking in the fresh mountain air.

Here, in Yosemite, I breathe in the present moment of peace, and step into the splendor of creation. Here, I realize that I am one with creation and her creatures, and I inherit the earth and enter the promised land. Here, I see that creation and peace are given freely to everyone along with the gift of life itself. Here, I discover myself in the peace of creation.

Yesterday, I stood for a while over a little clear creek next to a gigantic ten-foot-tall, gray boulder and watched a big, bright, blue-and-black Steller's Jay take a bath. This is one of my favorite birds, an enormous bright blue bird with a black head, with black feathers that come to a point on its head like a

Mohawk. He stood on a stone, jumped into the water, splashed around, shook his wings, then jumped out and looked around quickly to make sure he was safe, as if to make sure no one was watching. Then he jumped back in. I watched him jump in and out over twenty times.

In that private moment, I saw the sheer beauty, innocence, peace, and joy of creation, of life itself—the creek, the rock, the redwood trees, and the magnificent Steller's Jay. He was brimming with life, as were the waters, the rocks, and the redwoods. As is all of creation. It seemed so simple and clear, so obvious, the power and beauty and peace and shining reality of creation. All that is necessary is for us to open our eyes.

The day before, a lovely brown deer walked past my window in the early morning. I opened the front door of the cabin and stepped outside, and there she stood about twenty yards away. She looked right at me, and then started walking toward me. She came to a stop about eight feet in front of me, totally peaceful and unafraid. She looked at me for a while, and when she realized that I had no food, started on her way again. A moment of perfect peace. An eternal moment of oneness with creation and her creatures.

This afternoon, while walking in the green meadows below Half Dome rock, five brown deer walked right pass me. I stayed with them for forty-five minutes, watching them graze. On another evening, I saw five male deer grazing in the green meadows. The grass was about three feet tall, and since they were sitting down in the grass, enjoying something to eat as the sun set, all you could see were their large antlers sticking up in the grass.

Antlers in the grass. Another image of peace, beauty, and life.

Earlier, on my walk along the foot of the falls, a bear came running right across my path. He wasn't a cub, but he wasn't a full-grown bear either. He was light brown, almost blond, with dark brown legs, and full of energy and life. He ran past me and everyone else before we even realized he was there. He darted up to the base of the mountain and entered the woods. I watched him stand on a log, catching his breath, in the safety of the tall trees, before he sauntered away.

On Sunday morning, just before Mass, I walked out into the woods behind the visitor center to collect my thoughts, when a bobcat came up to me. He looked at me, turned his head, and sauntered on. Neither of us was afraid. We took account of one another and then went about our business. Or maybe we were in right relationship with one another. We both seemed quite at peace, and I took that as another sign of unity and possibility.

Yosemite is the first of our national parks, with over three million acres of the High Sierras set aside, and one of the most beautiful reserves in North America, if not the whole world. The deep valley with its rivers and creeks cuts through enormous granite cliffs for some fifteen miles, ending in front of the domineering Half Dome. Millions of people visit each year. My cabin is located just near the base of Yosemite Falls. I step out my back door and look straight up at the majestic Upper Falls, the highest waterfall in North America. Farther down, those waters turn into the rushing Lower Falls.

Today, in mid-May, the falls are full after a snowy winter. There has been no water falling for the past seven years, because of the California drought, but this spring, they are bursting as never before. Across the river and the meadows, and on the other side of cliffs, Bridalveil Falls comes rushing over the top of the cliff like a faucet turned on full.

Two miles down the road stands the granite wall of El Capitan, the world's largest exposed rock wall. Walking past it the other day, I could see eight climbers about halfway up the towering rock wall. El Capitan is daunting and overwhelming, but the rock climbers make me worry. I prefer to walk in the meadows, along the Merced River, to listen to the birds and the waters and breathe in the fresh air in perfect peace. There's no need to walk the cliffs or walk on water for that matter. Walking on the earth is exciting enough for me. At the moment, half of El Capitan is closed to all climbers so that the glorious peregrine falcons can nest and raise their young in tiny niches in the rock wall. They take priority, as they should.

This is not my first time to Yosemite. In 1969, my parents took my three brothers and me on a cross-country train trip from Washington, DC, to New York City to Chicago, to the Grand Canyon, Los Angeles, San Francisco, and Yosemite. Looking back on that memorable trip, I remember being stunned most of all by the New Mexico landscape. The tracks still stand today, less than a mile from my house, as the Amtrak train continues to pass through the remote New Mexico wilderness.

I was ten, but it really was the trip of a lifetime, and Yosemite was the goal. My father in particular was determined to see it. We stayed at Yosemite Lodge, down the path from where I'm now living. We walked these same paths, strained our necks looking up at these same majestic walls and falls, and touched the glorious sequoias and ponderosas. I still have pictures from that trip, and treasure one of a beautiful bear I photographed walking next to a sequoia. Yosemite has been with me ever since. It's always been part of my life.

There have been many other trips—to the Grand Canyon, the Redwoods, the Rocky Mountains, Canyonlands and Arches in Utah, Ghost Ranch in New Mexico, the beaches of Hawaii, the inlets and glaciers of Alaska, and, of course, the Outer Banks of North Carolina, where I grew up, near Kitty Hawk. But I always seem to come back to Yosemite. In the late 1980s and early 1990s, while living in Oakland and studying theology, I visited Yosemite with my friends regularly. The day before I left California, my friend Tom Hoffman and I spent a magical day walking from one end to the other, taking it all in. About ten years ago, I went camping by myself for a few days in Yosemite. Today, Yosemite feels like a second home. Actually, it's everyone's home.

As I walk through Yosemite Valley and take in the fullness of creation, I try to listen, to be aware, and to be mindful and attentive. I let go of my worries, concerns, problems, and issues, and enter as fully as I can into this paradise. It's like stepping into the Garden of Eden. One wants to be fully present, to have a heightened consciousness and awareness of the beauty that surrounds us. It is all gift. For me, Yosemite, like the other natural wonders of the world, bears the fingerprints of the Creator. It is a sign of God's presence, but it is also a summons, a calling, a responsibility. Yosemite, like all of creation, is alive and ever changing. It is pure wilderness, pure wildness, but it is vulnerable, too. We cannot make it, but we can destroy it, and once we do, it's gone forever. Like the earth itself, Yosemite hangs in the balance. It begs us to wake up, receive its gift in peace, celebrate the Creator together in peace, and do our part to stop the ongoing destruction of the earth.

When I come to Yosemite, I turn my back on the culture of violence and war and step into the new life of peace and resurrection. But there's more. In Yosemite, I enter that promised land of peace, reserved for the meek, the gentle, and the nonviolent. I'm not claiming to be worthy of such a blessing, but I recognize it and name it for what it is. It is pure gift, and I accept it with gratitude, peace, and an open heart and mind.

In Yosemite, we see how everyone can inherit the earth. But that gift requires a change of heart, a new intention, a deliberate turning. From now on, we must go forward, back into the world of violence and war, to do our part to end the killing, the suffering, and the ongoing destruction of Mother Earth. Yosemite, along with all of creation, calls us to wake up, stand up, and stop the insane destruction of the earth before it's too late.

A Time of Catastrophic Climate Change

If we are nonviolent, Jesus teaches, we will inherit the earth and become one with creation.

If we are not nonviolent, we will not inherit the earth, we will not become one with creation, and we will eventually destroy the earth and her creatures.

Jesus taught this basic truth two thousand years ago, and now we are seeing how right he was. Because we have practiced violence—global structured, institutionalized violence—and created systems of total violence, we have hurt and killed one another and destroyed the creatures and the earth. With the onslaught of climate chaos, we have entered the full consequences of global violence.

Today, we wage some thirty wars; possess some 16,000 nuclear weapons; support unparalleled economic inequality, corporate greed, and extreme poverty for over three billion people; and maintain a global epidemic of violence rooted in racism, sexism, and the oppression of the poor and disenfranchised. With our global rejection of Jesus' way of nonviolence, and our global pursuit of nature's resources at any expense, we have reversed the direction of creation and set off catastrophic climate change.

Gas emissions, temperatures, and sea levels have risen dramatically, and extreme weather now threatens us all. With the fossil-fuel industry digging up the earth, as well as the methane released by cattle who are being fattened for America's meat industry, we are filling the atmosphere with carbon. Temperatures rise, the ice caps melt, the seas rise, the storms get bigger, and the violent reaction of Mother Earth begins. We have bulldozed the forests and the Amazon, harvested the ocean of its fish, destroyed the soil and the vegetation, killed the coral reefs and poisoned the waters. We are killing the earth, but it will not go down without a fight. Total catastrophic climate violence is the normal, predictable, scientific response.

The last few years have easily been the hottest on record. Each year the record is broken all over again. We have witnessed unprecedented hurricanes, tornadoes, superstorms, rainfall, floods, tsunamis, fires, and droughts. The polar ice caps and glaciers are not just melting, they are disappearing. The global temperature has now risen about one degree Celsius (over the last hundred years), and already drastic changes are under way. The world's nations are talking about allowing a three-degree Celsius rise in temperature (about seven or eight degrees Fahrenheit), and that itself is a recipe for disaster. James Hanson, perhaps the world's leading climate scientist, insists that we can only let the world's temperature rise up to 1.5 degrees Celsius. But since he said that, it has already happened.

By the turn of the next century, sea levels will have risen at least seven inches, possibly as high as twenty-three inches. The earth will be ten degrees Fahrenheit warmer. Half of the world's population currently lives within thirty-seven miles of the sea, and three-quarters of all large cities are located on the coast, according to the United Nations. They will all be dramatically affected. Sea levels are rising three to four times faster along parts of the United States' East Coast than they are globally. There will be no ice in the Arctic (the first ice-free Arctic summer will occur by 2040). There will be no polar bears, no coral reefs, no Marshall Islands. Bangladesh, Florida, Manhattan, and other low-lying areas will be under water. The American Southwest will be uninhabitable because of the 130-degree heat and permanent drought. California's long drought could lead, for example, to a massive wildfire that burns Yosemite to the ground.

Scientists predict one hundred new wars over water and land during this century. Hundreds of millions will be forced to flee their homes, with at least 250 million new refugees by 2050. Nearly every person will live in poverty because of the loss of livable land and drinking water. Billions will die needlessly; many more will suffer. Scientists describe a hellish reality that is hard to imagine but inevitable unless drastic changes are made immediately.

Just before the COP 21 Climate Change Conference in Paris in December 2015, Pope Francis told a group of reporters that the world is now on the brink of committing "global suicide." "We are at the limit of suicide," he told reporters on November 30, 2015. In Pope Francis's 2015 encyclical *Laudato si'*, the most widely discussed and acclaimed papal encyclical in history, he lamented humanity's destruction of the earth and called everyone to take responsibility to stop that destruction. "Once we lose our humility, and become enthralled with the possibility of limitless mastery over everything, we inevitably end up harming society and the environment," he wrote.

Pope Francis challenged world leaders and ordinary Catholics and Christians to take bold new steps to protect the earth for future generations. People around the world have taken hope from his prophetic call, especially young people, and many millions are becoming more engaged in the struggle to protect creation. Francis has become a prophetic voice urging us to make the connections, care for the earth, and do what we can for the future. He calls us to turn back to the Creator and his intention for creation, and in doing so, invites us to reclaim the nonviolence of Jesus and to inherit the earth as a promised land of peace.

Nonetheless, Donald Trump won the 2016 presidential election, pulled out of the Paris Accords, and announced his intention to stop every effort to protect the earth. He wants instead to serve the fossil-fuel industry, indeed to dig for fossil fuels in our national parks. On that tragic election day, the World Meteorological Organization released a report announcing that the years 2011–2015 were the hottest on record, "with hundreds of thousands of deaths likely due to global warming from human activity." The report found human-induced climate change was directly linked to extreme events, including an East African drought and famine in 2011 that claimed over a quarter-million lives, and the 2012 Superstorm Sandy, which caused $67 billion of damage in the United States.

The climate science news continues to worsen, and yet the U.S. government, the fossil-fuel industry, the mega corporations, the superpowers and their militaries carry on with the same ol' same ol' politics of total greed, total war, and total destruction.

We have now become the ancient people who ate and drank and went about their business while Noah boarded his ark as the rains began to fall.

In Yosemite, when we gather for Sunday morning Mass, I invite the congregation to notice how Yosemite points us back to the Creator, to the fullness of peace, and, in the process, how it helps us recover our humanity and sanity so that we can return to our true selves, our best selves, to become again who we were meant to be, people of peace at one with creation and one other. Make your visit to Yosemite a time of prayer, reflection, and renewal with the God of peace and creation itself, I suggest. There are only a hundred tourists at each Mass, along with a handful of locals, but each Eucharist becomes an epiphany moment within the context of Yosemite, and I sense that people suddenly wake up to the wonder of the present moment in creation.

The locals are now my friends—the janitor at the post office, the painter at the Majestic Hotel, the bus driver, the tour guide, a few rangers, and others. They all have chosen a radically simple life in order to live out their days in Yosemite Valley. In the process, they have learned to let go, step into the present moment, and become one with creation. They don't know it, but they are little Buddhas, little saints, serving Yosemite and her guests, honoring creation and the Creator, ordinary holy environmentalists.

One evening, I visited with Ron Kauk, one of the leading rock climbers in the world. Since he was a kid, he has lived in Yosemite, over forty-five years now. He has been featured in *National Geographic* and stood in for Tom Cruise in one of the *Mission Impossible* movies, which opens with Ron hanging from a rock, thousands of feet above a desert floor. A film about him, *Return to Balance*, plays regularly in the Yosemite visitor center.

"I'm interested in learning how to become more human from nature," he told me. By living in a remote campground with few possessions over the course of many decades, he says he knows now that we are all one family, that we are one with nature, that life flows through him and the birds and the deer and the bear, but also the trees and the river and the rocks. Once a local Native American elder told him to live full time in "the miracle of life," and he has spent his life trying to do that, to be fully alive in the reality of Yosemite and the miracle of life.

"Yosemite is a center of peace," Ron Kauk told me one Friday evening. The natural world is trying to get us to slow down, to be calm, to be at one with one another and creation, to feel the peace of the present moment. Ron said this is how we are all called to live, at one with creation, in the peace of the present moment; and even if most people reject that gift, he was determined to spend his life fully alive in the miracle of life.

Every Saturday evening during summer, the church locals and scores of tourists gather at one of the farthest campgrounds for outdoor evening Mass at the large outdoor amphitheater. Half Dome stands right behind us, across Mirror Lake, bearing down on us. As the sun sets, we lift our prayers, our songs, and our hearts to the Creator in thanksgiving for this beautiful creation and the blessings of life, love, and peace. We hear the Gospels, receive communion, and pledge to carry on the journey of life in a spirit of peace, love, compassion, and nonviolence. We promise to become Yosemite people, mindful of creation and one another, stewards of this present reality, this present moment of peace. We are sent forth, in other words, as peacemakers.

Walking through Yosemite, one of the great centers of peace, I feel the majesty of creation and experience oneness with the earth and her creatures. I also recognize the impending doom of catastrophic climate change, the horrors that our corporate greed and systemic violence will unleash upon humanity and creation. I watch the sunset over Half Dome, listen to the waterfalls, and see the deer grazing in the tall grass. I remember how peacefully Jesus walked upon the earth and recall his wisdom of nonviolence.

I take a deep breath, and find the strength and the courage to go forth in his footsteps, the footsteps of peace and nonviolence, to live in the present moment of peace with creation, and to do what I can with others to stop the destruction of the natural world.

For thousands of years, indigenous peoples have been living that call, that life. They have always reverenced Mother Earth, studied the air and water and the land and her creatures, and learned from creation how to live in right relationship with one another.

Today, the indigenous peoples of the world continue to reverence the earth. But more than ever, at this critical moment in history, they are calling all of us to wake up and learn that same respect for Mother Earth and her creatures that we might not destroy creation but slow down climate change and live in peace with Mother Earth and finally discover all the gifts the Creator has left for us. With their wisdom in mind, I set off to visit my friend Marian Naranjo, a leading indigenous environmentalist, to listen to her wisdom.

Chapter 6

Marian Naranjo's Journey with Mother Earth

Recently, I set off from the mesa to spend an afternoon with one of the greatest environmentalists I know, a deeply spiritual woman who is an elder in her indigenous community and who has spent a lifetime enjoying and defending Mother Earth. I drove north toward Española, onto the sacred land of the Santa Clara pueblo. Located along the slowing, shrinking Rio Grande, the pueblo sits just below the mountain of Los Alamos, home of the Nuclear Weapons National Laboratories, where all our nuclear weapons are built. Today, the whole area has become a dangerous radioactive waste dump.

For hundreds of years, this peacemaking indigenous community lived at one with their holy land. Then Oppenheimer and the U.S. military stormed through, stole their land and mountains, built their nuclear weapons, and dumped their nuclear waste down onto the community below. The pueblo is the second poorest county in the United States, but the mountaintop and its evil labs are the second richest county in the United States, with one of the highest per capita rates of Ph.D.s and millionaires anywhere on earth. For seventy-five years now, the indigenous people along the river have suffered poverty, oppression, radioactive waste, and the full threat of the U.S. military. Their land and water have been thoroughly poisoned, and yet the Tewa, the people of the pueblo, continue their journey of meekness, gentleness, and nonviolence, and so, they live at one with Mother Earth.

Driving down Highway 30, just below the Los Alamos Mountains, I turn left onto the Santa Clara Pueblo, drive over the cattle guard onto a dirt road into a neighborhood of small, ordinary adobe homes. I drive along Flower Road and find her little adobe house with the turquoise trim on the corner.

In 2015, Marian spoke at the Campaign Nonviolence national conference that I organized around the time of our peace vigils at Los Alamos, marking the seventieth anniversary of the U.S. atomic bombings of Hiroshima and Nagasaki. She joined the likes of civil rights leader Rev. James Lawson, social scientist Erica Chenoweth, activists Kathy Kelly and Medea Benjamin, Buddhist teacher Roshi Joan Halifax, and many others in making the case for a new culture of peace and nonviolence. She spoke of her pueblo's long-suffering history and urged us to do what we could to stand in solidarity with them and the land. Over the years, she founded and directed Honor Our Pueblo Existence (HOPE), Communities for Clean Water, and their Youth Council Initiative Project. For decades, she has actively addressed environmental, health, and women's issues for her region, her pueblo, and her land.

It's a hot August day, and a normal busy day for Marian, what with her four children and seven grandchildren, and her many responsibilities around the pueblo. But she welcomes me with open arms and settles down on her couch to share her reflections. First, she says, let's pray. With that, she whispers an ancient prayer in her Tewa language, which she tells me holds all the advice passed on to her indigenous community since its earliest days.

"Right here on this land," she says at the start, "stood one of the largest volcanoes on the face of the earth, a super volcano. From its eruptions, life formed and evolved. We were the first people, the Towa, who were planted here. That is how our creation story arose. From those early times, we were taught how to walk and conduct our lives. The gift of the Creator for us is to walk on earth and to respect our air, water, and land. Our duty as indigenous here is to take care of the air, water, and land, and give thanks for them, because if we don't, this land is not going to take care of us. That's how our mannerisms formed. Our prayers, our dance, our songs all mention these gifts of air, water, and land. And so we respect them and walk on Mother Earth and survive.

"Indigenous people are all around the earth," she continues. "All these people are beginning points. Our creator stories connect with our mannerisms. We all have our own creator story, in the spirit world, and the job is grounding our story on the earth. We make mistakes because we're not in the spirit world, yet our energies come from there and go back there. Everybody has indigenous roots somewhere. Everyone needs to learn their own indigenous roots, to know the land where they come from, and to see what shape the land is in, and the air and water."

She tells me of her parents, how they were part of the Santa Clara Pueblo, how she was born on a U.S. military base in Utah, where her father was in the military. She traveled back and forth from Utah to northern New Mexico, and so, she explains, so grew up in both worlds and knew both worlds. "My childhood here was very happy," she says with a smile. "We lived in an adobe house. There were ten of us. We learned about privacy, how to respect each other, how to eat simply by growing our own food. Because I was one of the few who knew English, I was taken to sell things on the Santa Fe plaza. When I was a teenager, I started a youth organization, to help the other youth, who struggled because they did not speak English.

"We grew up with cultural events, our ceremonies, and the church, and we were one with Mother Earth. They helped me and everyone to know the difference between right and wrong, and how not to be hurtful. Our traditional ceremonies reminded us of air, water, and land."

Over the years, she tells me, she became a mother, and then a potter, so she could work at home, and in the process, she began to learn and make the connections. She had a wise mentor, a spiritual person, who helped her and many other teachers along the way. Working with the clay all day long became a daily meditation. She was working with air, water, fire, and earth, and so she naturally became an environmentalist.

"Working with the earth connects you," she says. "The earth is in your hands, it's in your mind. The earth grounded me spiritually. Because of the teaching to care for the air, water, and land, she grew. She worked with the earth as a potter for forty years. But when she was a teenager, with her high academic marks in math and science, she was chosen to go to Kentucky to participate in some science experiments, involving radiation. Just after high school graduation, she was offered a job at the Los Alamos nuclear weapons lab. She worked there for a summer, and was offered a well-paid, permanent, lifelong job. But she knew it wasn't right, so she quit and became a potter instead.

Decades later, as arthritis began to sit in, she climbed her sacred mountain one day to offer a prayer for guidance. "Here I am. What do you want me to do?" she asked in prayer. "I knew I couldn't be a potter any more. The very next day, a friend came over and invited me to lunch in Santa Fe." "Let's go to this meeting," he said. "We walked into a meeting of Concerned Citizens for Nuclear Safety, which was concluding an agreement with the labs about compliance with the Clean Air Act. I met them, and through the course of the settlement, I was hired as the first native outreach director for Concerned Citizens for Nuclear Safety." At the same time, she was offered a job to do outreach on the environment for eight northern New Mexico pueblos.

And so, she began to read the stacks and stacks of environmental reports about the Los Alamos National Laboratory, and how it had systematically poisoned their sacred land. She was the first indigenous person in New Mexico to read line by line the government reports about the poisoning of the land, air, and water from radioactive waste. She started copying page after page and taking them to her tribal leaders. No one knew the depth of what had been happening.

After twelve years of hard work, she was able to get one pueblo village to comment to the government about these environmental documents. She helped an attorney write the statements of behalf of their tribal council, to protect their air, water, and land. It was the first recognition of a government-to-government relationship, she said, and it was on behalf of Mother Earth.

"I had asked my elders for permission to do this work," she told me. "I asked them, 'How do we feel about the Los Alamos labs being on our sacred place?' I asked everyone this question and I found that everyone had a story to tell. It was as if they had all been holding it in for a long time. I started to go to all the pueblos and speak with all the elders about Los Alamos and its effect on our land and our people.

"Then one day, I was called into a meeting of the leaders of the eight pueblos. They told me I was 'intervening,' and I was fired. I told them I didn't need their paycheck, and went back to work. Now, after all these years, at a recent meeting with the pueblo governors, I found them in prayer, offering thanks that they were able to stand up to the Los Alamos labs on behalf of Mother Earth." She has had a quiet but transformative effect among her people, helping them work with others to prevent further destruction of the sacred landscape of northern New Mexico.

I didn't understand how the male pueblo leaders could quietly go along with the labs' destructive work over the decades. "We were a conquered people," she said sadly. "The U.S. military people did not ask permission to come here. Through the War Powers Act, they gave themselves permission to do whatever they wanted to do. Our people couldn't fight that. We had waged a war long ago, and it's taken three hundred years to coexist peacefully now with Hispanic people. So we decided to become our enemies. I speak English. I'm my enemy. People had jobs at Los Alamos. We had federal dollars coming in. It's all about money. They didn't want to take on Los Alamos because of the loss of money and jobs. But now, we are beginning to remember who we are.

"Today, we are remembering who we are. We *are* this land. As we remember who we are, we are granted the courage to speak the truth, with love and care and help. In the face of climate change, we can change our mannerisms. We all have to change our manner of living. If people are willing to do this, we can hold hands and do it together. Everything can be done differently. We can change to solar energy. It can all be done. We are receiving the courage to do things right.

"We have this holy sacred place. This was our heaven on earth. Now this negative force is here, the labs, with the power to end all life. It's up to the people to make conscious decisions, to find the right balance with everything. If we don't, it will all end."

I ask her about nonviolence, and the beautiful third beatitude with its mysterious connection between nonviolence and inheriting the earth. "Nonviolence is a mannerism of love, care, helping, and respect, which was at the center of our ancient teaching. It's so simple, yet we don't do this. The culture of domination wants to own everything; it does not love or respect anyone or anything. Our villages have been undergoing incredible suffering because of the culture of domination. Violence is all around us now—drugs, alcohol, addiction, jailings, and deaths, right here. So with nonviolence, the question for us is: how do we heal ourselves of these things? Part of my job as a woman elder is to teach my community how to heal ourselves. It's happening, just slowly, not overnight. We are starting to learn how to heal ourselves.

"I also cofounded Los Mujeres Hablan, 'The Women Speak.' We've been following the Los Alamos historical assessment retrieval project. The Center for Disease Control did a report on the Trinity Test, the first nuclear explosion, in Alamogordo, in July 1945. Now the National Cancer Institute is starting phase two of the study, to research radiation exposure to the local people, the Hispanics, the native peoples, the ranchers. This is the first government study since July 1945.

"Years ago, the big fire in our mountains meant we lost our watershed, so we changed what we do. Now we use ground water; we are not dependent on the mountain stream. We are starting again to connect with Mother Earth. Water is such a powerful force. I helped cofound 'Communities for Clean Water' because of the known pollutants from the Los Alamos labs. We are addressing our water. We file lawsuits, we sit down at the table with the labs and the governments, and we make them get permits from us and settle with us. The latest successful permit was for storm-water runoff. Now they have to legally ensure that no pollutants are coming down the mountain or the river into our water.

"I think we're all witnesses," she reflects. "We watch what people of aggression are doing. Poverty, oppression, and the culture of domination make us humble and meek. So our people are pure spirits. Creator recognizes pure spirit. Oneness with the earth is part of our direct line with the Creator. So we weave our way through this negative mess and survive and do what we can with love, care, respect, and help for others. Your mannerism and how you walk on the earth reflect your oneness with the earth.

"That's why it's important to recognize place," she continues. "This is one of the major indigenous sacred places on the whole earth. As we acknowledge it, it affects our decisions, how we walk on earth. This has to be taught, learned, and practiced. People in the United States need to recognize place. Once place is recognized, the mannerisms of one's daily life begin to change. The people of the labs came to this place and disrupted so many things on the earth—with the mining, with not putting back what they took, with greed, disrespect for others, not knowing the true meaning of love, and always helping themselves instead of helping others. That's what our capitalistic culture and leadership are all about. All that has to change.

"If we can recognize place and Mother Earth, we can start to undo all this. The recent economic crash was a sign. If something catastrophic happens again, we will all be forced to change for our survival—to live simply, eat locally, and become friends with our neighbors. We need to continue our planting, to care for the water, to treat each other respectfully if we are going to survive. We all have to learn this or we will all perish.

"Eleven years ago, I helped cofound the New Mexico Food and Seed Sovereignty Alliance. Every spring we gather with farmers from all over the state in a different community—one year a pueblo, the next a Hispanic community, and we have prayer, ceremony, seed exchanges, blessings, meetings, and sharings. We are coming together, learning together, and preparing together."

I ask her to sum up her message. "Here's the essence," she says. "We all need to be in the process of great healing. We need healing from our past in order to be present now in knowing where we are, who we are, so that we can all make conscious decisions about how to go forward for future generations, so we can walk peacefully on earth." She smiles.

She walks me to the door, and together we step outside into the hot, sunny August day. We look up at the massive white clouds, and it starts to rain even as the sun continues to shine. "See," she says, gesturing to the panoramic sky. "Our land is paradise, and our goal is to return it to the 'heaven on earth' it was intended to be, not to let it be 'hell on earth.'"

Just then, the rain starts to pour and pour, harder and harder, a relentless, sheer downpour. And before our eyes, the rain turns to hailstones. And the hailstones fall twice as hard. We stand there and watch this marvelous event. All the while, the sun continues to shine. After a minute or two, as quickly as it started, the rain and hail begin to stop. The sun shines on.

"See?" Marian turns to me and asks with a smile. "We are so blessed."

CHAPTER 7

Berta Caceres, Martyr for Mother Earth, Presente!

Defending Mother Earth in this time of unparalleled corporate greed, imperial military might, and human-made catastrophic climate change is a matter of life and death. For some of us, death will come sooner rather than later, in the form of horrific storms, mudslides, floods, tornadoes, fires, and drought. For others, death will come at the hands of the multinational corporations and their government-backed death squads who destroy the earth, steal its resources, crush the poor, and kill their advocates. And yet, those who stand with the earth and suffering humanity in a spirit of nonviolence will be greatly blessed with the fullness of life.

In 2015, at least 116 environmental activists were killed, three-quarters of them in Latin America.[1] The following year, the *Washington Post* published a special investigation called "For Latin American Environmentalists, Death Is a Constant Companion," which began with a list of recent deaths:

> A young worker who protected sea turtles in Costa Rica was kidnapped and brutally beaten. A farmer in Peru was shot 12 times for protesting a hydroelectric dam. A Guatemalan activist who linked a massive fish kill to pesticides sprayed by a palm oil company was gunned down near a courthouse in broad daylight. A Brazilian activist who fought

logging in the rain forest was ambushed and fatally stabbed while returning home with his wife. The common threat in virtually every case is the fight by communities to stop government-approved corporate development of remote lands. Slain environmentalists frequently have attempted to halt such projects as dams and logging involving hundreds of millions of dollars, which stand to enrich local providers of labor and materials. Most victims "are indigenous people who are oppressed, largely marginalized and are considered almost expendable by the powers that be."[2]

Honduras in particular is one of the deadliest countries in the world to be an environmentalist, according to the group Global Witness. At least two environmental activists were killed each week in 2014. The best known of all those killed in recent years was Berta Caceres, who was killed by two government-backed assassins in her modest home in La Esperanza in the middle of the night on March 3, 2016. She was shot four times. A Mexican activist who was staying with her was shot twice. He pretended to be dead. After the assassins left, he went over to Berta, and she died in his arms. The authorities blamed him for the killing and detained him for several weeks. In my opinion, he was released only because of international pressure.

Berta Caceres was a world-renowned environmentalist of the Lenca indigenous people of western Honduras. She spoke out publicly and fearlessly against the destruction of the Honduran environment, for the rights of her indigenous community, for justice, and for an end to the corporate takeover of the earth by multinationals and their government-backed death squads. In 1993, she cofounded the National Council of Popular and Indigenous Organizations in Honduras, or COPINH. She organized hundreds of protests and campaigns to prevent dams from being built, to stop oppressive logging and mining operations and to reclaim ancestral lands for the indigenous. At the time of her death, she was organizing an aggressive public campaign against a dam being built by the world's largest dam builders that would have hurt the local economy, displaced indigenous peoples, and destroyed much of the natural region. In her last years, she was under constant harassment and the threat of death, but she refused to back down. Though she knew her fate, she never stopped working for the earth or her people. She gave her life for the poor, for justice, and for the earth.

"They fear us because we're fearless," she would say.

"Berta was unflappable," her friend activist Beverly Bell wrote. "She was calm in the face of chaos and strategic in the face of disaster. She was indefatigable, working around the clock with no complaint. When not traveling around Honduras or the world to raise support for the struggle, she would wake early and go straight to her desk to receive updates, often on the most recent attacks on COPINH members, and in those cases, to write condemnations — all even before a cup of coffee. She would then jump into her yellow truck to pick up other members of COPINH and head off to wherever action or investigation was needed."[3]

For Berta Caceres, the struggle itself was one; all the issues were connected. She embodied the connections. For her, life was a nonviolent struggle on behalf of her indigenous community and all indigenous peoples, but that meant it was a struggle on behalf of their land and the earth itself. But given the forces of violence arrayed against her and her people, that meant she had to resist capitalism, racism, and patriarchy. Her struggle led her across Honduras, Central America, and the world. She met grassroots and political leaders everywhere, including Pope Francis. In 2015 she was awarded the prestigious Goldman Prize, the leading environmental award in the world.

"We come from the Earth, from the water and from corn," she said in her acceptance speech. "The Lenca people are ancestral guardians of the rivers, in turn protected by the spirits of young girls, who teach us that giving our lives in various ways for the protection of the rivers is giving our lives for the well-being of humanity and of this planet. Walking alongside people struggling for their emancipation, COPINH validates this commitment to continue protecting our waters, the rivers, our shared resources, and nature in general, as well as our rights as a people.

"Let us wake up!" she concluded. "Let us wake up, humankind! We're out of time. We must shake our conscience free of the rapacious capitalism, racism, and patriarchy that will only assure our own self-destruction. The Gualcarque River has called upon us, as have other gravely threatened rivers. We must answer their call. Our Mother Earth, militarized, fenced-in, poisoned, a place where basic rights are systematically violated, demands that we take action. Let us build societies that are able to coexist in a dignified way, in a way that protects life. Let us come together and remain hopeful as we defend and care for the blood of this Earth and of its spirits."[4]

"She was bold, utterly bold," my friend Jean Stokan told me. Jean and her husband, Scott Wright, have spent the past thirty-five years working for justice and peace in Central America. They knew Berta for fifteen years. "She stood up to anyone and any power," Jean continued, "and spoke out in front of politicians and military men with rifles. She named and unmasked what was happening and the lies behind it. She was an extraordinary leader, driven by love. She was a deeply spiritual person."

"The latest destruction of Latin America is because of extraction. The multinational companies are coming in and taking everything—every mineral, every natural resource, every piece of land that can yield a profit. After the coup in Honduras in 2009, there was an international conference in Honduras called 'Open for Business.' That's what this struggle is about: business trumps human rights and the environment. That's what Pope Francis is speaking about when he says that the profit motive should never come before people's lives. Berta was clear about the connection between unbridled capitalism, violence, oppression of the poor, and the destruction of the land. She questioned why the land is being destroyed and the model of development that prioritizes profits over people and their land. That's why some have called Berta a *Laudato si'* martyr."

"For Berta, the words of *Laudato si'*—'the cry of the earth and the cry of the poor'—were one cry," Scott Wright told me. "I had known her over the years through the struggle for justice and various campaigns. The day after she was killed, I flew down to Honduras for her funeral, and it was there, in her hometown, that I realized how deeply connected her identity was with the earth. The indigenous are the first defenders of the earth, because their identity is connected with the earth. These big projects—the dams and mines—were not only threatening the environment and their culture, but their identity. I had a sense that day that the fate of the earth in a spiritual sense is in the hands of the indigenous.

"Berta was deeply compassionate," Scott continued. "She was a fierce fighter. She didn't mince words. She spoke truth to power. She confronted the military on many occasions, and always from a posture of nonviolence. In one YouTube video, she talks about slipping into the river and the river told her to keep going with the struggle, to have courage, that one day her people would win. Archbishop Romero said that the martyrs of El Salvador were killed because they got in the way. That's what happened to Berta. She was killed because she got in the way and kept getting in the way. She got in the way of the mining companies, the dam companies, the multinational corporations, the army, and the government. Her name appeared on a death list. Berta knew she was going to be killed, but she kept working anyway."

I asked Scott what we can learn from Berta's life, struggle, and death. "Berta was a martyr," he said, "and now she is part of the cloud of witnesses. She was a *Laudato si'* martyr, who gave her life for the earth and the poor. The cry of the earth and the cry of the poor are one cry. All of us have a responsibility to cherish, reverence, protect, and defend the earth for the sake of vulnerable communities, particularly the indigenous, but also for the future. If the earth is no longer sustainable, then the future is no longer sustainable."[5]

After her death, people took to the streets in Honduras and the United States, calling for an independent, international investigation, justice in Honduras, and a suspension of all military aid to the Honduran security forces. They carried signs saying, "Berta didn't die, she multiplied." Hundreds pledged to carry on where she left off, to continue the long struggle for justice, peace, and environmental sustainability.

Berta Caceres exemplifies heroic commitment for Mother Earth and her indigenous peoples. Like all the *Laudato si'* martyrs, she embodies the beatitude of Jesus, who connected nonviolence and the struggle for justice with oneness with the earth. There have been hundreds, thousands, perhaps hundreds of thousands of martyrs like her. They call the rest of us to take up that struggle where they left off.

Few of us will be killed like Berta Caceres, but all of us can do our part to resist systemic injustice and catastrophic climate change. Like Berta, we can step up to the plate, speak out publicly for climate justice, make the connections, join the grassroots movement, side with the earth and her suffering people, and give our lives as best we can for a more just and peaceful future.

Great martyrs like Berta Caceres show us the way. Inspired by their courage, we can take a new step forward and do our own part for the earth, and live out the beatitude of Jesus.

CHAPTER 8

Taking a Stand at Standing Rock

Like millions of other concerned people, I followed the standoff at the Standing Rock Sioux Nation in North Dakota throughout 2016. The good people of Standing Rock, including the Dakota, the Lakota, and the Sioux, have stood their ground since April 2016, to block the evil 1,170-mile, $3.7 billion Dakota Access Pipeline, which will dig through the three-mile-wide Missouri River, potentially poisoning the water for hundreds of thousands, perhaps millions of people, and desecrating the sacred land of the indigenous people. They've built several large camps and a permanent campaign that has gained the support of two hundred other tribes.

Thousands made the journey to Standing Rock to stand in solidarity. The Obama administration told the Army Corps not to issue the permit for drilling under the river, but the preparations continued. Hundreds of unarmed peaceful people have been arrested in acts of nonviolent civil disobedience. State police and brutal pipeline security guards have attacked the nonviolent people with dogs, mace, tear gas, and rubber bullets and consistently lied to the media, blaming the peaceful people for their violence.

Through it all, the Native American people have stood and walked in a steadfast spirit of prayer and nonviolence. Before our eyes, they demonstrated that rare kind of *satyagraha* reached by Mahatma Gandhi, Dorothy Day, Martin Luther King Jr., and the finest nonviolent movements in history. In doing so, they exposed for all the world to see the centuries-old racist war on Native Americans and the equally centuries-old war on the earth itself, as well as the power of creative nonviolence when wielded properly.

After months of confrontation, a national call to clergy went out. Clergy were summoned to drop everything and get to Standing Rock for a day of prayer and repentance, and a march from the main camp to the bridge where the police and pipeline security officials block the road to the notorious pipeline construction site.

And so I went. Over six hundred women and men priests and ministers from various Christian denominations made the journey, along with hundreds of other activists, in late October 2016. It was one of the greatest experiences of my life.

Looking out from the plane over the barren prairies of North Dakota, I was startled by the massive bright blue Missouri River. It is much bigger than I realized. From the air, it was so clear to see that, indeed, "Water Is Life," as the Standing Rock saying teaches. Our plane was packed with church folk and young activists, and so was the Bismarck airport. There was excitement and hope in the air. Solidarity seemed alive and well.

As I drove south under the big blue sky across the rolling brown prairies to the village of Cannon Ball near the Standing Rock camp, the orange sun began to set, and the sacred landscape radiated beauty, energy, and life. I walked into the packed gymnasium for the evening orientation and nonviolence training and found a hushed standing-room-only crowd listening attentively to Father John, the local Episcopal priest who has served here for twenty-five years, as he explained the scenario for the next day. Several Standing Rock leaders spoke before food and refreshments were offered. It was clear from the get-go that nonviolence was the order of the day.

They call themselves "protectors" not protesters, "pray-ers" not disrupters, "peacemakers" not "troublemakers." It's that creative nonviolence that has attracted the interest and sympathy of people around the country and the world.

The next morning, I drove to the Oceti Sakowin camp as the sun rose over the mysterious North Dakota landscape. From the hills above the camp, it looked like a sea of tents with the striking exception of the scores of large white teepees sprinkled throughout the camp. It was a sight to behold. The Cannon Ball River ran along one side of the camp, and large, brown rolling hills circled the entire area in the distance. Here, for the past months, thousands of people have maintained a nonviolent *satyagraha* campaign to protect the land, the water, and the dignity of the Standing Rock people.

At 7 a.m., as I approached the main gathering place for worship, I noticed the large billboard with the camp rules: "We are protectors. We are peaceful and prayerful. We are nonviolent. ISMS have no place here. We respect the locals. We do not carry weapons. We keep each other accountable."

There, around the Sacred Fire, several dozen Native women offered morning prayers and then set off for the daily walk to bless the water. Over the next two hours, hundreds of clergy, mainly women and men Episcopal priests, arrived and greeted one another. Over the course of the day, we exchanged stories, shared our feelings, and plotted strategies for future solidarity. I was happy to see friends Ann Wright of Voices for Creative Nonviolence, Rev. Lennox Yearwood of the Hip Hop Caucus, and Bill McKibben of 350.org.

At 9 a.m., Father John began a liturgy of prayer and repentance, where we formally denounced the ancient "Doctrine of Discovery," the church document from the 1490s that empowered European authorities to steal the land and resources of indigenous peoples. After silence and prayers, it was burned in the Sacred Fire. Then the march began.

We set out from the camp, by now a thousand of us, well over half in various clerical church attire, with black robes, white collars, and colorful stoles. Most of us carried bright posters that read "Clergy Stand with Standing Rock."

We walked slowly, mindfully, peacefully down the main road, over the hill, and down toward the bridge, where the police had barricaded the road to prevent people from approaching the actual drilling and construction site of the pipeline. We sang as we walked—"Amazing Grace," "This Little Light of Mine," "We Are Marching in the Light of God." It was one of the greatest, most peaceful marches I have ever experienced in a lifetime of marching for justice and peace.

When we reached the bridge, we gathered together for songs and speeches. A wonderful African American woman minister led us in "The Water Is Wide." A group of Jewish women sang an inspiring prayer in Hebrew. A young Quaker activist read her congregation's statement of solidarity. Another Native elder and minister prayed for the pipeline workers, police, and security guards, and the coming day when they would join our circle and together we could celebrate creation and the Creator.

In my speech, I thanked the Standing Rock people for their steadfast resistance and exemplary nonviolence, and reflected on Jesus' connection between nonviolence and oneness with the earth. I recalled his teaching in the Beatitudes, "Blessed are the meek; they shall inherit the earth," and noted that meekness is the biblical word for nonviolence.

Long ago, Jesus connected nonviolence with oneness with the earth, I said. We have forgotten that connection, rejected nonviolence as a way of life, supported the culture of violence, and now are faced with the consequences of systemic violence—the destructive pipeline and catastrophic climate change. But the Standing Rock people are calling us back, I continued. They urge us not just to reject the pipeline, honor their land, and protect our water, but to reclaim our common nonviolence and shared oneness with the earth. They are showing us the way forward, and it's time for more and more of us to follow their lead.

More songs, speeches, and prayers followed, and then everyone exchanged the sign of peace. Bag lunches were offered, and people sat down on the tall brown grass to eat, talk, and rest after the day's march.

Later that afternoon, a hundred clergy drove north to Bismarck for another protest at the state capitol. Fourteen were arrested inside during a sit-in, calling for an end to the pipeline and for respect for the Native lands and water.

But I stayed back and spent the rest of the day walking through the main camp, meeting and listening to hundreds of people. It was a powerful experience, to encounter so many people who were coming together in this difficult but beautiful campaign.

One young Standing Rock couple with two little children showed me their video from the demonstration the day before, when police and pipeline security officials sprayed the people with tear gas and shot them with rubber bullets. Others told me about the military-style raid on another camp the previous week, which led to the removal of everyone's meager possessions and the arrest of 140 protectors. The pictures could be from our military maneuvers in Iraq, Afghanistan, Yemen, Palestine, Libya, and Pakistan. More, this war against the indigenous people and North Dakota landscape is not new: for one thing, hundreds of nuclear weapons have been planted in this sacred ground, ready for takeoff and global destruction.

One Native elder, who was also an ordained United Church of Christ minister, reflected with me on the possible outcomes that lay ahead, including the Obama administration's effort to move the pipeline many miles north. In the medic tent, one young Native physician's assistant told me stories of previous demonstrations, their care for the marchers and their basic mission—"to keep people alive."

I visited the artist collective, various kitchens, tents where extra clothes were being collected and given away as needed, and the media tent. In another tent, I came upon the daily nonviolent direct action training, required of every newcomer on the day of their arrival. Some 150 people were being trained in the basics of nonviolence. It was the civil rights movement all over again.

As I stood and watched a group building the geodesic dome in the center of the camp, it was clear: they may be cold, but they are on fire.

The next day, I read an editorial in the *New York Times* calling for the pipeline to be moved far away from Standing Rock. It said in part:

> A pipeline may well be the most profitable and efficient way to move a half-million barrels of crude oil a day across the Plains. But in a time of oil gluts and plummeting oil prices, is it worth it? Is it worth the degradation of the environment, the danger to the water, the insult to the heritage of the Sioux?
>
> The law-enforcement response to the largely peaceful Standing Rock impasse has led to grim clashes at protest camps between hundreds of civilians and officers in riot gear. The confrontation cannot help summoning a wretched history. Not far from Standing Rock, in the Black Hills of South Dakota, sacred land was stolen from the Sioux, plundered for gold and other minerals, and then carved into four monumental presidential heads: an American shrine built from a brazen act of defacement.
>
> The Sioux know as well as any of America's native peoples that justice is a shifting concept, that treaties, laws and promises can wilt under the implacable pressure for mineral extraction. But without relitigating the history of the North American conquest, perhaps the protesters can achieve their aim to stop or reroute the pipeline.[1]

Perhaps. If the Standing Rock campaign is some day able to stop or reroute the pipeline, it will do so because of their steadfast nonviolence and the strong movement that has grown up around them. Despite the Trump administration's unjust support of the pipeline, the movement continues and everyone is needed to support their grassroots nonviolence on behalf of Mother Earth.

"It is essential to show special care for indigenous communities and their cultural traditions," Pope Francis urges. "They are not merely one minority among others, but should be the principal dialogue partners, especially when large projects affecting their land are proposed. For them, land is not a commodity but rather a gift from God and from their ancestors who rest there, a sacred space with which they need to interact if they are to maintain their identity and values. When they remain on their land, they themselves care for it best."[2]

Standing Rock is a sign of our predicament, and a sign of hope. We can continue the legacy of racism, oppression, corporate greed, war, and environmental destruction and hasten the worst of catastrophic climate change, with the Trump administration—or we can all become earth and water protectors, Standing Rock people of nonviolence.

Standing Rock offers a path beyond the stale politics of corporate media, corporate greed, and corporate violence. It demonstrates the best of our humanity. We can all become people of peace, prayer, earth, and water; people who care for one another in community, who share our resources with one another, who learn from creation how to live in peace together as the Creator intended.

With the people of Standing Rock, perhaps we can discover new strength to stand up for what is right, for a future in solidarity with Mother Earth and one another, for a new world of nonviolence. If we open our hearts and join hands, as our sisters and brothers of Standing Rock have done, maybe we too might catch fire. Maybe our hearts will burn with a passion for Mother Earth, and we too will give our lives to protect her and creation.

CHAPTER 9

A Global Movement for Mother Earth

Each year, we experience higher temperatures, more droughts in some regions and more rainfall in others, the shocking ice melt and superstorms, and catastrophes we could never before imagine, and each year, millions of ordinary people take action to protect Mother Earth and future generations. We buy the correct new light bulbs, put in new solar panels, become vegetarians, shop locally for organic food, recycle everything, walk and bicycle more often, avoid plastic, conserve our water, and plant a garden.

But now we know: that's not enough. We need to keep fossil fuels in the ground, end carbon emissions, and protect the oceans, the forests, the creatures, and the environment as much as we can. To do that, we need to build political willpower on behalf of Mother Earth and thus a strong, powerful global grassroots "people power" movement to stop environmental destruction, first of all by the fossil fuel industry, and create a new nonviolent world where Mother Earth and her creatures, along with our impoverished children, receive our upmost attention.

"We need a new and universal solidarity," Pope Francis wrote in *Laudato si'*. "All of us can cooperate as instruments of God for the care of creation, each according to his or her own culture, experience, involvements and talents."[1]

Bottom-up grassroots movements are the only way real positive social change has happened historically, from the abolitionists and the suffragists to the civil rights movement and the antiwar movement to the women's movement and the environmental movement. An active global grassroots movement of nonviolence on behalf of Mother Earth is the only way to stem the worst of climate chaos and the insane greedy politics that allow it. Any positive steps that have been made to date are due solely because of the steadfast local and global movements that have resisted environmental destruction and fought to protect Mother Earth. Even as the fossil fuel industry and its corporate, military, and government sponsors dig in for further insane catastrophe, our global movement has to dig in as well, and broaden and expand to include as many people as possible. Together, we can build a kind of global Marshall Plan for creation. That will require the awakened participation of every human being. Everyone is needed. As Pope Francis writes, everyone has a gift and a talent to bring. Everyone can be Rosa Parks, that tipping-point person who breaks the global grassroots movement wide open for Mother Earth.

The global environmental movement has been building for years. From the creation of Earth Day, to the growing development of renewable energy through solar panels and alternative transportation such as electric cars, to steady protests at fracking installations and oil pipelines, to steadfast campaigns pushing political candidates to address the reality of climate change, we continue to push for the change that the science, the truth, the times demand.

Case in point: the initial Keystone XL pipeline victory. This particular pipeline went from western Canada all the way to Texas, bringing the dirtiest, most dangerous Tar Sands oil to ships in the Gulf. Commissioned in 2010, it was a done deal. There was nothing that could be done, according to general wisdom. In 2011, author and activist Bill McKibben asked NASA scientist James Hansen for his assessment. If the Keystone XL pipeline is allowed to happen, he said, "It's game over for the planet." With that dire warning, Bill issued a national call: Do everything you can to stop this pipeline. Speak out, lobby, organize, agitate, protest, even engage in civil disobedience if necessary: this pipeline must be stopped.

There was nothing that could be done, and yet thousands began to organize and mobilize. On November 16, 2011, thousands of people circled the White House to urge President Obama to take action. About 1,200 people were arrested in one of the largest civil disobedience actions in decades. In February 2013, 50,000 people marched in Washington, DC, to stop the pipeline. In March 2014, 400 were arrested in front of the White House in a protest against the XL pipeline.

Then, after six years of review, in 2015, President Obama announced he would not approve the Keystone XL pipeline. It would never provide the jobs that Republicans promised, but more importantly, it might tip the balance toward the worst of catastrophic climate change. That 2015 victory showed how grassroots nonviolent people-power movements can take on the fossil fuel industry and force an unthinkable policy change. There have been others: the "kayakistas" who blocked Shell Oil drilling ships getting to the Arctic in time from Seattle, the ongoing campaigns to outlaw fracking, and the growing divestment movement. The price of solar panels has fallen 80 percent in the last ten years. Bangladesh will be fully solar by 2021. People are beginning to buy electric cars. Norway will allow only electric cars in a few years. Change is under way.

Then on September 21, 2014, 425,000 people marched through the streets of New York City in the largest climate change gathering in the history of the world. Once again, Bill McKibben issued the call. That summer in an article in *Rolling Stone,* he wrote that climate change was "the biggest crisis our civilization has ever faced," but that the People's Climate March "would be the largest demonstration yet of human resolve in the face of climate change." "A loud movement," Bill wrote, "one that gives our 'leaders' permission to actually lead, and then scares them into doing so—is the only hope of upending the 'prophecy' that it's already too late to reverse the problem."[2]

Throughout the summer, people made plans to get to New York or organize their own local solidarity march. In July, I was invited to join the national steering committee for the peace contingent of the march. There were to be six contingents, each with its own stage, featuring indigenous people, environment groups, young people, labor and anticorporation groups, interfaith groups, and our antiwar, pro peace/pro earth movement. We held national conference calls every Friday morning for months. The plan was to gather that Sunday morning in September at 8 a.m. for our own particular rally, hear from speakers and musicians, then join the march south through Manhattan. I invited Congressman Dennis Kucinich and Bill McKibben to speak, and folk singers Dar Williams and Peter Yarrow to perform. They all agreed.

The city had closed off Central Park West from Columbus Circle to the high Nineties by setting up chain-linked fences on all sides. The march was set to begin at 11 a.m., but by 8 a.m., we knew already that the projections were way off. A massive crowd had already gathered. Our flatbed truck with our sound system in the back was prevented from entering Central Park West. So we stood on the back of another truck near our West Eighty-sixth Street entrance and took turns speaking through a bull horn to tens of thousands of people. Peter Yarrow and Dar Williams stood in the middle of the street, as the crowd made space around them, and launched into the great movement songs of old. Everyone started singing along with them as if we were some new kind of environmental Occupy movement. But by 11 a.m., the crowd was so tight, pressed shoulder to shoulder, that panic began to spread, and we worried that people would get crushed. Just then, the people ahead of us started to move south. The march had begun and off we went.

It was overwhelming, exciting, and inspiring, full of spirit and hope and positive people-power energy. My friend Patty and I walked on ahead toward the front of the march to see it all for ourselves. We went through huge contingents of marchers—impassioned youth groups, colorful indigenous people, labor groups, church groups, Buddhists in robes, and so forth. They sang, chanted, danced, and cried out on behalf of Mother Earth. At the front, Al Gore, Jane Goodall, Bill McKibben, Leonardo DiCaprio, and others smiled and walked slowly forward. It was the largest march of its kind, with an additional 2,600 solidarity marches and events held simultaneously around the world in over one hundred nations. With that march and those actions, the people of the world spoke up and climate change was now on the global agenda.

"Global warming is a structural and systemic problem," Bill McKibben told a recent interviewer. "Until now, we've allowed ourselves to pour carbon for free into the atmosphere—to use the heavens as an open sewer. That needs to change. And for real change to happen the most important thing that we as individuals can do is to stop being individuals for a while, and to join together and organize! . . . We need to build movements that are themselves a form of community. We have enormous issues to address. In order to address them, we need strong movements of people demanding action."[3]

Many thousands of indigenous, environmental, labor, and faith groups work every day to build a global grassroots movement on behalf of the earth. In terms of activists, Bill McKibben stands out. He has been organizing and speaking out for decades, and written many influential books, including *The End of Nature* and *Earth: Making a Life on a Tough Planet*. A professor at Middlebury College in Vermont, he cofounded the global environmental action movement www.350.org, which has organized to date over forty thousand demonstrations worldwide.

"Last year, we learned that the great West Antarctic ice sheet has begun an irreversible melt, and the waters of our ocean planet are rapidly acidifying," Bill said in 2015. "Summer sea ice in the Arctic is largely a thing of the past. When the biggest features on earth are being remade in just a matter of years, that is a bad sign. And of course we can see it close up in the endless siege of extreme weather—drought, flood, storm, and the other phenomena we once called biblical."[4] "Truthfully, it scares the hell out of me," he confessed. "It's happening faster than even the most dire predictions suggested."[5]

"It's a race, and we have a chance," he said. "The movement that people have built has begun to give us a chance. But we have to push harder than we've ever pushed before—against politicians and those who pull the strings, the rich companies. The fight is with the fossil fuel industry. We are engaged in a fight about money and power and the fossil fuel industry has everything. We had to figure out how we were going to match them, and with the movements, the passion, the creativity, and the willingness to go to jail, it has started to work. We haven't lost yet. This work has given us the chance to keep on fighting. If we do it right, we will preserve the ability for the next generation to keep on fighting. Our hope is to keep on fighting. We need to engage as intensely as ever."[6]

"What fascinates me about Gandhi and Martin Luther King Jr. is not only the clarity of their moral visions," he said, "but the power of their tactical acumen. These two qualities are not unrelated. Their insight from the Sermon on the Mount— that one heaps coals on the head of one's adversary when one returns kindness for enmity—is invaluable. It underlay the fall of the British Empire in India and the fall of Jim Crow in the United States."[7] "But unlike past struggles, with climate change, it's a timed test. If we don't change our ways quickly, it won't matter. In this case, God has given us a blue exam book, and when a certain amount of time has passed, we have to put our pencils down."[8]

In this movement, he notes, there are no leaders. "We have no Dr. King. We're just a huge sprawling resistance movement in the face of the fossil fuel industry and we know how to unite when we need to unite. We continue to build strong coalitions. I don't know if we are going to win this fight, but I do know that we're going to fight. In every corner of the world, people are coming together to figure out what to do and how to fight."[9]

"I imagine more of us will need to go to jail in the years ahead," Bill said.[10]

And then Donald Trump was elected president, promptly cut every act for the protection of the environment, and pulled out of the Paris Accords, "a stupid and reckless decision," Bill McKibben wrote the next day in the *New York Times*.[11] The nonviolent resistance would have to be stronger and more widespread than we'd ever imagined.

"The good news is that we've built a big movement," Bill McKibben said the day after Trump's election. "The bad news is that it's clearly not big enough yet. So I guess the main task at hand is to keep building the movement."[12]

That will require civil disobedience, he argues. "We need to use our bodies to block deportations and pipelines," he insists. "We also have to remind our nation what it looks like to turn the other cheek, not with resignation but with courageous calm. By speaking with their sacrifice, *satyagrahis* (nonviolent truth seekers, à la Gandhi) remind us what it means to be fully human and fully engaged. At its most powerful, civil disobedience changes the atmosphere. It may not convince the active oppressors to change their ways, but it can shift the *zeitgeist*. And not just around the issues, but around the way we pursue those ends. The more beautiful our response is, the more powerful it will be."[13]

The day after the November 2016 presidential election, the Sierra Club issued an equally strong call to carry on the struggle. "We will fight and resist," executive director Michael Brune wrote. "We will not cower in a defensive posture for the next four years. We've fought against long odds many times before and won. Remember that our Beyond Coal coalition defeated one coal plant proposal after another during the Bush presidency. Trump can't stop regulators and local governments from choosing clean energy when it's the cheapest and smartest option. [His administration] can't stop cities from going to 100 percent clean energy. They can't stop the private sector that wants to be part of the climate solution, not the problem. They can't stop millions of people from exploring and protecting our precious public lands. Cities, towns, and states will be the leaders on climate and environmental protection for now. We'll have to adjust many of our strategies, but we won't allow our progress on climate and clean energy to be stopped. We can't afford to give up or waver from our conviction to fight for climate action and against corporate polluters. In the months and years ahead, we will redouble our campaign to fight the fossil fuel industry and to make sure that our climate and communities are protected."[14]

And so, we build up the global environmental grassroots movement; resist our politicians, war makers, and fossil-fuel corporations; deepen our active nonviolence; and stand with Mother Earth, come what may. We all have to become, like Jesus, Mother Earth protectors.

CHAPTER 10

Connecting the Dots through Campaign Nonviolence

Catastrophic climate change is the natural consequence of global systemic violence. That means, it is intimately connected with racism, sexism, classism, militarism, war, nuclear weapons, and every form of violence. If we want to deepen our nonviolence and our conscious oneness with the earth, we have to connect the various facets of systemic violence with environmental destruction so we know what we are up against, what we are resisting, and how broad our creative nonviolence needs to go.

If we want to live at peace with Mother Earth, we will have to broaden creative nonviolence in every possible direction as conscious loving sisters and brothers who love one another, who love everyone, so that we live more and more at peace with ourselves and one another. Perhaps then, we will begin to make peace with Mother Earth and her beautiful creatures.

All-encompassing nonviolence requires constant vigilance against every form of violence, resistance against every structure of violence, and strategic, mobilized action in every direction for a more nonviolent world. Perhaps we best take a moment to reflect on these aspects of violence, their nonviolent alternatives, and the broad creative nonviolence that connects the dots, if we want such a nonviolent world to come true.

Racism, Sexism, and Classism

Structural systemic racism means that white people oppress people of color not just through personal and group prejudice but through legal systems, structures, and institutions that perpetuate this global social, political, and economic injustice. One of the many deadly consequences of systemic racism at home and abroad is environmental racism. We see this, for example, in the North American toxic waste dumps that are placed disproportionately close to people of color; in the drastic disproportionate effect of extreme weather and climate change on the world's indigenous peoples, the ones least implicated in its cause; and most generally, but most predominantly, in the poorest nations of the Global South who bear the disproportionate brunt of extreme weather and climate change, even though, again, they are least to blame. Confronting and ending systemic racism at home and abroad will require deepening our nonviolence and recognizing every human being as a beloved brother and sister in order to learn how also to respect and protect Mother Earth.

Systemic sexism has forced the world's women to be hit hardest by catastrophic climate change. Women, especially women of color, women in poverty, and women of the Global South, suffer far greater disadvantages around the world than men, find themselves stuck in a permanent rut, and often fight daily for their survival and their children's. As climate change hits the world's poorest with floods, hurricanes, typhoons, tsunamis, droughts, and fires, it hurts women, and their children, first of all. The work to end sexism, educate women, and get them out of abject poverty empowers them to fight the causes of climate change, protect the earth, and build more nonviolent societies for the future. Empowering women to lead us in peace means putting Mother Earth first and working to end her destruction.

Likewise, structural systemic classism means in general that very, very poor people, the four billion people who struggle to survive every single day on one or two dollars, will suffer and die fastest from the consequences of catastrophic climate change—that is, compared to the wealthy one percent of men, white men, the one percent of the one percent who own the vast majority of the world's money and resources. In the face of extreme weather, the super rich fly off in their private jets to higher ground while the suffering poor are left to die. This global injustice is now played out regularly. We've seen it during Hurricane Katrina in New Orleans, Matthew in Haiti, tropical cyclone Winston in Fiji, typhoon Yolanda in the Philippines, and Harvey, Irma, and Maria in the Caribbean. It will become the story of the future, as hundreds of millions of people are forced to flee as homeless refugees. This chaos will lead to further violence, poverty, and warfare—unless we stand up together and press the world's wealthy elite to give their resources back to the poor and disenfranchised on behalf of all humanity and Mother Earth.

I remember flying to Haiti in October 1992, where I spent a month meeting with church groups across the country during the coup that ousted President Aristide and then testified to a U.N. commission. From the plane window, I could see the shimmering green/blue ocean, and then the island of Hispaniola, with miles of green trees and jungle making up the eastern half, the Dominican Republic.

But then, all of a sudden, there was a sharp line right across the whole island, where everything west turned brown. That was Haiti from the air. The desperate poverty drove people to chop down every tree in the nation for firewood. Without trees, the island turned to dirt and mud, setting itself up for greater environmental destruction, poverty, and death. Even from the air, Haiti was shocking.

The super rich need to spend their billions not on greater wealth but on humanity so that we can abolish systemic poverty, create climate justice, and educate everyone in the methodologies of nonviolence. A few billionaires, like Bill Gates and Warren Buffett, are beginning to do this, but that is not how change predominantly comes. Everything and everyone has to change. There should be no more billionaires, no more starving people, no more daily struggle to survive. Everyone everywhere should have adequate food, clean water, housing, health care, education, employment, and dignity so that together we can resist climate change; create more nonviolent, more egalitarian societies; and protect Mother Earth and her creatures. Everything has to change.

People of color, women, children, and the world's poorest people suffer the hardest effects of climate change. Syria might be a case in point. A historic decade-long drought drove millions of rural villagers in Syria to the cities over a decade. That massive mobilization led to social unrest, which led to revolutionary, violent fervor and warfare and eventually the systemic killings of nearly a half-million people. Did climate change lead to the suffering and death of hundreds of thousands of Syrian women and children? It certainly laid the groundwork for total war. The U.S. war making and military occupation throughout the Middle East helped as well. Instead of creating more just societies and funding nonviolent conflict resolution, we bombed infrastructures, killed millions, and funded systemic injustice throughout the region.

Syria may become the norm for the future if we do not reverse our war-making trajectory, fight the roots of climate change, and institutionalize nonviolent conflict transformation. Indeed, we need to do everything we can as people and nations to end racism, sexism, and classism, so that we can learn to live in peace and work together to mitigate the unimaginable suffering and impending horrors of catastrophic climate change.

The Transforming Spirit and Global Struggle of Active Nonviolence

To overcome racism, sexism, and classism, we need to recognize that every human being is our very beloved sister and brother. This is the heart, soul, and spiritual vision of non-violence—that we are all one, all reconciled, all sisters and brothers of one another. If we are white, and raised in a racist culture against people of color, we need to fight against our own inner prejudices and against the evil systems that legitimize and create racism by naming every human being as our beloved sister and brother and working for racial equality and justice. If we are men, we need to overcome our sexist, patriarchal upbringing and resist the structures of sexism and patriarchy to create a more equal society. Together, we try to create new structures that support and uphold every human being equally, regardless of their race or gender or any other distinction, and advocate for a more inclusive, nonviolent world.

If we do not speak out against systemic injustice and resist it, we remain on the side of systemic injustice. If we truly care for Mother Earth, we have to make these connections and publicly support the struggle for racial and gender equality, fully aware of how a more inclusive, just, and nonviolent society will extend to Mother Earth. As we advocate for adequate food, clean water, housing, health care, education, and dignity for every human being alive, for every sister and brother, and broaden our nonviolence, we show our care for our common home and extend the horizons of peace.

In particular, people of the Global North need to recognize their systemic privilege in the face of the extreme poverty and total disenfranchisement of the billions of suffering people in the Global South. That means, we need not only to give away our wealth to the world's poor and support the struggles of the impoverished, marginalized, starving masses for justice, but actively pursue a new, just global system of economic equality and redistribution of wealth so that no one starves and everyone has food, water, education, health care, employment, housing, and dignity. These are the basic human rights of every human being, and the fundamental vision of nonviolence. Pope Francis stressed this connection in *Laudato si'* when he emphasized that global capitalism was at the heart of catastrophic climate change, that the abuse of fossil fuels was driven by the corporate greed in reckless pursuit of infinite money. Capitalism, Francis points out, has failed. It has led to extreme poverty, permanent warfare, and now, catastrophic climate change that has the potential to wipe out all life on earth. We need to create new nonviolent societies, based on democratic socialism where everyone has an equal share, no one gets abused, and Mother Earth is treated with respect.

For us as North Americans, that means we need to make a preferential option for the world's poor and marginalized, to make reparations to the Global South, to think and act globally, and to pursue justice in all its forms everywhere around the earth for the sake of our sisters and brothers and the earth itself. Injustice anywhere, Dr. King taught, is a threat to justice everywhere. In the face of catastrophic climate change, the days of injustice need to come to an end. We need to eliminate every form of injustice in every corner of the world so that justice toward one another can lead to climate justice and create a more nonviolent world.

"Every ecological approach," Pope Francis writes, "needs to incorporate a social perspective which takes into account the fundamental rights of the poor and the underprivileged."[1] We need to "hear both the cry of the earth and the cry of the poor."[2] "In the present condition of global society, where injustices abound and growing numbers of people are deprived of basic human rights and considered expendable," Francis concludes, "the principle of the common good immediately becomes, logically and inevitably, a summons to solidarity and a preferential option for the poorest of our brothers and sisters."[3]

If we are ever to break through class, privilege, economic domination, and imperial oppression into a new world of social, economic, racial, and climate justice for all people, everyone will have to join the struggle. Literally, every human being on the planet now has to enter the struggle for justice and peace if humanity is to survive.

Abolishing War and Nuclear Weapons for the Sake of Mother Earth

Having named racism, sexism, and classism as key pillars of our culture of violence that serve catastrophic climate change, we still need to name the reality of war and weapons, and nuclear weapons in particular, as key ingredients of catastrophic climate change.

Though no one has ever declared it formally, powerful peoples, rich nations, and empires throughout history have long waged a permanent war on earth, one that has finally set in motion the earth's violent response. According to the laws of nature and physics, climate change cannot be stopped unless we engage in a full-on global effort to end its causes, reverse our direction, and respect Mother Earth. While that means ending our reliance on fossil fuels, it also means ending warfare itself.

Several years ago, I spent a difficult month traveling through war-torn Colombia, where over 200,000 people had been killed during their twenty-year war. Every day I journeyed with friends to a different village to meet with survivors of various massacres by government death squads, working in conjunction with the U.S. military and various multinational corporations to extract Colombia's vast resources at whatever price. People told us horrific stories of torture and executions by military officials working on behalf of North American mining companies and other corporations.

I will never forget riding along a mountain road and coming around a bend and seeing an entire mountain range that traveled across the horizon that had been totally deforested by a

Canadian lumber company. I knew about deforestation, but to see a wall of mountains stretching for miles, in one of the lushest, greenest regions of the world, with no trees on it, reduced to brown dirt, was shocking and devastating. Many thousands were killed so that lumber could be stolen, regardless of the consequences to Mother Earth. Colombia ranks third highest in biodiversity, and yet over the course of its war, the earth was destroyed over and over again.

"How greatly we need the Lord's strength to seal us with his love and his power to stop this mad race of destruction!" Pope Francis writes. "Destroying what he has given us, the most beautiful things that he has done for us, so that we may carry them forward, nurture them to bear fruit . . . The wars that continue do not exactly help to sow the seed of life but to destroy. It is an industry of destruction."[4] "Whereas God carries forward the work of creation and we men and women are called to participate in his work, war destroys. It also ruins the most beautiful work of God's hands: human beings. War ruins everything, even the bonds between brothers and sisters. War is irrational; its only plan is to bring destruction. It seeks to grow by destroying."[5]

If we want to protect Mother Earth, we need to stop bombing her and destroying her, which means we need to end all our wars. We need to stop paying for war, supporting war, sending young people off to war, promoting war, and making war inevitable. We have to abolish our nuclear weapons and weapons of mass destruction, which destroy and permanently poison the earth, air, and water, and, instead, fund and institutionalize international nonviolent conflict resolution and methodologies so that war becomes obsolete. All the evidence proves that nonviolent conflict resolution works when it's tried. What's lacking is the global political will to abolish war once and for all.

War kills and injures countless millions of sisters and brothers around the planet. It also destroys buildings, infrastructures, civil society, and the basics of human life. But further, it literally destroys the earth. It blows up the land, sets it afire, poisons the land, water, and air, floods it, or renders it uninhabitable for humans and other sentient beings, leading to greater dust bowls, droughts, and extreme weather. The trillions of dollars spent on warfare by the United States and other nations increases harmful greenhouse emissions and wastes unlimited energy.

It's hard to measure the environmental destruction caused by war, nuclear weapons, and the culture of militarism, but scientists agrees that militarism in all its aspects increases climate change. The International Peace Bureau lists a number of direct ways in which military activity affects our physical environment:

- Pollution of the air, land, and water in peacetime;
- Immediate and long-term effects of armed conflict (explosions, landmines, unexploded remnants, chemical weapons, burning oil wells, and oil spills);
- Land use (vast areas of land and water occupied by military bases, target ranges, weapon stores, training grounds; pollution and degradation from storage, deforestation, and scorched-earth tactics);
- Weapons development and production (design, development, manufacturing, tests, storage, transport, and disposal); and
- Militarization of outer space (rocket launches, missile systems and satellites, and space littering).[6]

For decades, we have let the weapons' manufacturers, war makers, and their fossil-fuel allies bomb, kill, and wreck the planet. This can no longer continue. We all have to noncooperate with the culture of war and the spirit of militarism and nationalism. If we want to protect Mother Earth, we have to abolish nuclear weapons and end war itself, and become people of total nonviolence. That is the teaching of Jesus' third beatitude, and now we are beginning to recognize this wisdom as our only hope.

Campaign Nonviolence: Modeling a Globally Interconnected Movement for Transformation

We need a global climate mobilization, like a new Marshall Plan, that will keep fossil fuels in the ground, end fracking and poisoning the land, air, and water, even change every building code so that solar panels are the new norm. We need to educate ourselves and put pressure on every elected official on earth to save the planet and her creatures. That means, we have to take the long view, as visionaries like Martin Luther King Jr. did.

"The choice is no longer violence or nonviolence," Martin Luther King Jr. told us the night before he was killed. "It's non-violence or nonexistence." That statement has haunted me and challenged me my entire life. These days, it plays out in every headline. If we want to survive, we all have to become non-violent, and we all have to work to create a more nonviolent world. That is the only sane choice left. That means, we need to create a bottom-up national and global grassroots movement of nonviolence for a new culture of peace and nonviolence.

A few years ago, the little peace group that I work with, Pace e Bene Nonviolence Service, launched Campaign Non-violence as a long-term grassroots movement to mobilize the nation and the world through the power of active, creative nonviolence. We knew from the get-go that we had to help people begin to connect the dots between war, poverty, racism, sexism, nuclear weapons, and environmental destruction. None of these monumental challenges can be solved separately, and all of them affect our relationship with Mother Earth, yet we continue to address them separately. We started Campaign Nonviolence as a new way for people to connect the dots between the issues, connect the dots between the organizations and movements that have been toiling separately for years, and to connect the dots even in the vision of a more nonviolent world—so that nonviolence is practiced by all people toward all people, for justice and dignity for everyone, including all creatures and Mother Earth.

Long ago, Dr. King outlined several basic principles of nonviolence that still hold true today: nonviolence is a way of life for courageous people; it seeks to win friendship and understanding; it seeks to defeat injustice, not people; it holds that voluntary suffering can educate and transform; it chooses love instead of hate; and it holds that the universe is on the side of justice. In his 1964 Nobel Peace Prize acceptance speech, Dr. King said: "I have the audacity to believe that people everywhere can have three meals a day for their bodies, education and culture for their minds, and dignity, equality, and freedom for their spirits." He went on to envision humanity overcoming war and bloodshed until "nonviolent redemptive good will" rules the land. He spoke of a new world of nonviolence that is actually possible, and he organized a strong movement to help make that happen.[7]

In the spirit of Dr. King's audacious vision, Campaign Nonviolence called on people across the United States to join together in a week of national action against war, poverty, racism, environmental destruction, and the entire epidemic of violence, and in pursuit of Dr. King's vision of a new culture of peace and nonviolence. We began with the week of September 21-27, 2014, when to our amazement, over 235 actions and events for justice and peace were held across the country in every state and every major city. Marches, rallies, vigils, prayer services, fasts, and festivals took place from California to Maine, from the state of Washington to Florida, and from Arizona to New Hampshire. Events also took place in Afghanistan, Colombia, and Canada.

The following year, our national conference in Santa Fe and our peace vigils on August 6, 2015, for the seventieth anniversary of the U.S. atomic bombing of Hiroshima outside the Los Alamos National Laboratory, birthplace of the atomic bomb, and again on Sunday, August 9, on the seventieth anniversary of the atomic bombing of Nagasaki were filmed for a wide YouTube audience and were featured in the *New York Times* and promoted on Twitter by Yoko Ono.

A month later, our second national week of action, September 20-27, featured over 370 events across the country. Tens of thousands of people attended public events, marches, rallies, and vigils against war, racism, police killings, drones, nuclear weapons, poverty, and environmental destruction, calling instead for a new culture of peace and nonviolence. Over 100,000 people followed us on social media.

Then, during September 18-24, 2016, over 750 events, actions, and marches were held across the United States, involving over fifty thousand people and one million viewers on social media. Ordinary people of all ages gathered in a spirit of nonviolence, connected the dots, and spoke out against racism, poverty, police brutality, war, drones, nuclear weapons, the death penalty, and environmental destruction, and continued the call for a new culture of peace and nonviolence according to the vision of Rev. Dr. Martin Luther King Jr.

In Chicago, Rev. Mike Pfleger led one thousand people on a Friday night march through the streets of the Southside, starting at the famous Saint Sabina Church, to call for an end to gun violence and killings. Many relatives of those shot dead in recent months joined the march. Friends in Wilmington, Delaware, organized thirty-seven events across the state—including marches, films, art exhibits, and meditations. "We started as a Campaign Nonviolence march for a culture of peace and nonviolence," June Eisley says, "and over the years became a statewide movement for a culture of peace and nonviolence."

Raleigh, Durham, and Chapel Hill, North Carolina, declared a "week of nonviolence"—with sixteen events—to combat gun violence, racism, Islamophobia, poverty, environmental destruction, and support for war. On September 21, people of faith and conscience came together for a noontime vigil in downtown Raleigh followed by a news conference to detail their week of events, including regional nonviolence training. They put on a Campaign Nonviolence Triangle Area Peace Festival on September 24, featuring an interfaith Walk for Peace to raise awareness about love, truth, peace, and nonviolence for everyone in the Triangle area. Each of the cities declared September 18-24 "Campaign Nonviolence North Carolina Week."

In Memphis, Tennessee, hundreds of people, black and white, young and old, gathered below the balcony of the Lorraine Motel, where Dr. King was killed, to begin the Memphis CNV Week of Action. Religious leaders of every denomination spoke for an end to all violence and called for Memphis to become a nonviolent city.

During the September 16–24, 2017, National Week of Action, over 1,600 events, marches, and vigils were held across the United States and the world.

Every single CNV 2016 National Week of Action event was documented (see www.paceebene.org), and we are going to continue organizing this national week of action until thousands of events take place and everyone joins the grassroots movement of nonviolence.

The Nonviolent Cities Project

Another way we are encouraging people to connect the dots locally and act globally is by pursuing a new vision of their community as a nonviolent city.

While speaking in Carbondale, Illinois, I learned that local activists had launched a city-wide movement under the banner and vision of "Nonviolent Carbondale." They created a website, formed a steering committee, set up monthly meetings, and launched Nonviolent Carbondale as a way to promote peace and justice locally. I thought what they did could be replicated elsewhere as a new way to build on Dr. King's vision and connect the dots locally.

Inspired by their efforts, Campaign Nonviolence launched "The Nonviolent Cities Project" and called on activists and community leaders across the United States to pursue a vision of their local community as a nonviolent city, along the lines of Nonviolent Carbondale. With this vision of nonviolence, people could begin to reimagine their communities and to see a path forward toward a more nonviolent future. Very quickly, leaders in over forty cities contacted us and decided to pursue this model and vision. We think this project offers a new next step in the visionary, organizing nonviolence of Mahatma Gandhi and Martin Luther King Jr., and people are responding to it.

The key feature of the Nonviolent Cities Project is that each city needs to connect the dots between its violence; address its violence in all its aspects, structures, and systems; and pursue a more holistic, creative, city-wide nonviolence, where everyone practices nonviolence, promotes nonviolence, teaches nonviolence, and even institutionalizes nonviolence on the local level in pursuit of a new nonviolent community. We want to undermine the local and regional culture of violence and transform it into a new culture of nonviolence.

That means that Nonviolent Cities Project organizers would work to promote this new vision, call for nonviolence to be taught and practiced at every level, and mobilize people in every corner to work together for a new nonviolent community and a new nonviolent future. That would include everyone from the mayor and city council members to the police chief and police officers, to all religious and civic leaders, to all educators and health care workers, to housing authorities, to news reporters and local media, to youth and grassroots activists, to the poor and marginalized, to children and the elderly. Together, they would address all the issues of violence and pursue all the angles and possibilities of nonviolence for their city's transformation into a more nonviolent community.

The first goal would be a rapid reduction in local violence and an end to killing. Nonviolent Cities would work to end racism, poverty, homelessness, and violence at every level and in every form; dismantle housing segregation and pursue racial, social, and economic nonviolent integration; end police violence and institutionalize police nonviolence; organize to end domestic violence and teach nonviolence between spouses and nonviolence toward all children; work to end gang violence and teach nonviolence to gang members; teach nonviolence in every school; help get rid of guns, gun shows, and local weapons manufacturers; pursue more nonviolent immigration programs and policies; get religious leaders and communities to promote nonviolence and the vision of a new nonviolent city; reform local jails and prisons so that they are more nonviolent, and educate guards and prisoners in nonviolence; put up signs calling for nonviolence everywhere in the community; address local environmental destruction, climate change, and environmental racism; pursue clean water, solar and wind power, and a 100 percent green community; and, in general, do everything possible to help their local community become more disarmed, more reconciled, more just, more welcoming, more inclusive, and more nonviolent.

Through the Campaign Nonviolence annual national week of action, our Nonviolent Cities project, as well as its ongoing nonviolence training and nonviolence education, we are trying to help people realize that the struggle is one, that everything is connected, and that nonviolence is our future. If more and more of us can join the struggle, connect the dots, take a stand, practice nonviolence, and see how every facet of life on earth affects Mother Earth, we can help make inroads of peace, cut the roots of war, lessen the violent catastrophe from climate change, and finally make peace with Mother Earth itself.

CHAPTER 11

Standing with Mother Earth in the Inner City

A few years ago, I was in Oakland, California, and stopped by to visit my friend Anne Symens-Bucher and the new community she and her family had started. The mother of five, a lifelong peace activist, and secular Franciscan, Anne, along with her husband, Terry, founded Canticle Farm, a peace and nonviolence community right smack dab in one of the most violent, run-down blocks in the country. They wanted to explore the connections between poverty, racism, violence, guns, prisons, war, and environmental destruction and seek a viable alternative right there in the thick of everything. They named their community Canticle Farm, after Saint Francis's hymn to creation.

Anne is no stranger to this work. In the 1970s, she lived with Dorothy Day at the New York Catholic Worker. In the 1980s, she founded the Oakland Catholic Worker, then later the Nevada Desert Experience, as a way to pray and protest nuclear-weapons testing at the Nevada Test Site. She worked for over twenty years as codirector of the West Coast Franciscan Office for Justice, Peace, and Integrity of Creation. Her children are now fifth-generation Oakland residents.

Over the years, Anne and Terry bought two houses next to each other in the Fruitvale section of East Oakland. Eventually Canticle Farm bought three more adjacent houses. Living on the fault line between two of Oakland's most violent gangs, they had long dreamed of an inclusive community of peace and nonviolence. They had no idea if it was possible or if it could work, but they took a leap of faith and started it.

Over the years, as an assistant to writer and teacher Joanna Macy, Anne met scores of young environmental activists. Some of them stayed at her houses of hospitality, sometimes for months at a time. Canticle Farm developed slowly, but after several months, they had fifteen community members living in five houses connected by a large backyard.

That backyard became the center point of transformation. Like every other house in the neighborhood, their little houses were separated by fences. To create a large organic garden, they had to take down the fences. They took down the fences, and the transformation began.

"When we took down the fences between our yards," Anne told me, "we were also taking down the fences in our hearts. That's when we really began to know and love our neighbors and make peace with one another. At the center was the garden. Mother Earth was transforming us."

They created a large organic garden as a way to make peace, restore the neighborhood, honor Mother Earth, and teach nonviolent living. Theirs is one of the most creative inner-city experiments in the country. Others like it are springing up everywhere.

Their goal, they told me over lunch, was to be a presence of peace and nonviolence in the neighborhood. They knew that making peace in inner-city Oakland meant going deep into contemplative nonviolence, and that meant somehow connecting with Mother Earth. They decided to hold hour-long silent meditation sessions every day. Some even kept silence on Mondays, as Gandhi did. They made a commitment to explore what restorative justice and reparations could mean in their racially diverse neighborhood.

Then they launched Canticle Farm Sundays. They started

with a Eucharistic liturgy. While doing this, they reached out to their neighbors and invited them to lunch and to help out with the organic garden. And they offered them seeds to start their own gardens. As they got to know their neighbors and heard their concerns, they began afternoon programs on various practical items such as cooking, growing medicinal plants, and making herbal medicines. In the process, their neighbors became their teachers.

"While we have a vision of what can happen," Anne told me, "we know it has to emerge from our connection with our neighbors. Our neighbors have skills and gifts to offer but few places for them to be appreciated. We started out thinking we had much to offer and discovered we had much to learn and receive from our neighbors. If we show up with open hearts and a desire to be of service, miracles will happen." The community started organically, she said, so they want to let it grow organically. And that's what's happened.

"Our real security is not in our fences or barking dogs," Anne told me, "but in our relationships. This is the way to peace. We have misguided 'warrior' energy in our neighborhood. Our young people are fighting and dying to protect their 'turf.' We want to suggest that 'the turf' is Earth Herself. These young people are our future and we need to invest in them. That means interrupting the street- and school-to-prison pipeline by creating meaningful work opportunities and supporting them with the mentoring of elders."

When I asked Anne about the motivation underlying her work, she immediately spoke about St. Francis. He served the poor, practiced nonviolence, built community, honored the earth, and made peace, right in the midst of violent Assisi. "I'm trying to embody that phrase attributed to St. Francis," Anne said, "Preach the gospel at all times; if necessary, use words." She read me her mission statement:

> Inspired by the life of St. Francis of Assisi, Canticle Farm is a community providing a platform for the Great Turn-

ing—one heart, one home, and one block at a time. The Great Turning—the planetary shift from an industrial-growth society to a life-sustaining society—is served by Canticle Farm through local work that fosters forgiveness in the human community and compassion for all beings. Canticle Farm primarily focuses on the poor and marginalized as those who most bear the burden of social and planetary degradation, as well as being those who are first able to perceive the need for the Great Turning. Rooted in spiritual practice, Canticle Farm manifests this commitment by engaging in the "Work That Reconnects," integral non-violence, gift economy, restorative justice practices, urban permaculture, and other disciplines necessary for regenerating community in the 21st Century.

"We know about peak oil and global climate change, how the system is coming apart," Anne says, "so we try to help each other get ready for the future by growing our own food and taking care of one another. We could go to the neighbors and say, 'The end is coming, so start growing your food and get ready,' or, we could say, 'Let's grow our own food now because it's fun and in the process, we can share it with one another, get to know one another, and build a safer and beautiful community.'"

"We're in this fix because somewhere we got disconnected," Anne notes. "We got indoctrinated into thinking that we're separate from nature, that we're better than nature. Increasingly, the outdoors are something we travel through from one building in a vehicle to another building. If we are going to create a life-sustaining culture, we need more than holding actions. We need to wake up and realize that we're alive in earth, not on earth, that we are not separate from earth. We are living, breathing members of the living body of Earth.

"We want to act on behalf of earth because what's happening to earth is happening to us," she says. "What we're doing here is providing the whole experience. We need to restore right relationship with everyone and with Earth. So we feed people from the garden and share the seeds and encourage other gardens to be built. It's all about reconnecting—reconnecting with Earth, with one another, and with ourselves, with how we live, what we eat, what we wear, and what we do.

"What can we learn from the outdoors if we just pay attention?" Anne asks, quoting the poet Mary Oliver. "Right in our lives we have a rhythm that we've gotten disconnected from, that can teach us so much. What happens to the garden, the seasonal cycles, our bodies? What happens if we let things die, outside and inside of ourselves, if we give ourselves over to the rhythm of the garden?

"Our community has become a little oasis," she says. "People pour out their love here. That love is a force more powerful than the forces of destruction. And there's peace here. It's being cultivated. From the original people of this land, something of the sacred is still present, so we are nourishing it. We're cultivating a place of love, peace, and nonviolence in an urban environment where there's a lot of violence. When the neighbors come, and see the garden and chickens, something happens. We invite them to eat and share the food growing in the land, to sing, meditate, and make new friends. The tragedy is that so many are disconnected from earth and where the food comes from."

"Nonviolence isn't just a philosophy of resistance, it's a way of life," another community member tells me over lunch. "Nonviolence includes the thoughts we have, the words we use, the clothes we wear, the things we eat, the things we do. It's not just the absence of violence, not even just the absence of wanting to cause harm. Nonviolence is a state when your heart is so full of love, compassion, kindness, generosity, and forgiveness that you simply don't have any room for anger, frustration, or violence."

The other day, he said, he ran into three neighborhood kids—ages fourteen, fifteen, and sixteen—who were probably gang members, and welcomed them into the community and showed them around the main house. As he took them into the large meditation room with its white carpet, freshly painted white walls, and large green hanging plants, one of the kids said, "I feel so peaceful here."

"That moment," he said with a smile, "when we helped facilitate peace and harmony in the heart of that local teenager was worth all our effort."

These days, the community includes three men who have been paroled after serving over twenty-five years in prison. With their help and power, Canticle Farm has become a nonviolent presence in a violent neighborhood, a place of peaceful hospitality, restorative justice, and earth-based living. Through their intentional living, gardening, community, and nonviolence, they point a way out of violence, a way forward into a new life of nonviolence.

"We took down the fences and started growing food," Anne says with a smile. "That's how we did it, and that's what everyone can do. We don't want others to say, 'This is wonderful but I could never do this.' On the contrary, we want everyone to figure out how they can take down the fences in their hearts and relationships, grow food together with their neighbors and gift it, and in the process, create an oasis of peace wherever they live."

Wonderful, indeed. Canticle Farm is teaching us that even in the inner city, we can inherit the earth.

Chapter 12

A Down-to-Earth Spiritual Life

The dirt path up into Box Canyon is not long, perhaps only a mile or so. This hidden place is one of my favorites. Located in northern New Mexico, beyond Santa Fe and Abiquiu, it's nestled between the towering red, orange, and yellow cliffs of Ghost Ranch. As you walk through the trees, bushes, and rocks, you enter upon an open space of pungent, low-lying sage brush with strange massive walls of red, orange, and yellow rock. There is no sound, only perfect silence, except for the occasional black raven flying overhead, squawking, telling you to get lost and go home.

I walk through the field of sagebrush up to edge of the red cliff, and find a boulder and sit on it. I look out at the field of gray sagebrush that spreads before me, with the massive cliff wall looming behind me. To my left, half a mile away, stands the giant red-rocked Kitchen Mesa. On my right, the strange yellow and orange cliffs circle around and eventually meet up with Chimney Rock, with Georgia O'Keeffe's house settled far below.

Straight ahead in the far distance, twenty miles away, a blue mountain range keeps watch. In the center stands the Pedernal, an unusual mountain that gently slopes upward on its left and right side, until it reaches a flat table top, like Table Mountain in Cape Town, South Africa. Georgia O'Keeffe loved the

Pedernal and painted it again and again over many decades. "If I painted it enough," she said with a smile toward the end of her life, "God told me I could have it."

I take a deep breath. The big blue cloudless sky surrounds me, and the sun shines down upon me. It's mindfulness made easy. Suddenly, I am one with creation, with the beauty of Mother Earth. I am completely still, all at once at peace, breathing in the pristine air of the high desert. I become the consciousness of Mother Earth. I can sit here forever, a new-fangled, post-modern, radical Christian Buddha, ignored by the world, but transfigured by creation and her Creator.

As we face the reality of catastrophic climate change, people ask, "Where is God in all this?" God has forgotten us, we think. God wants us to suffer and die and destroy the world. God is on the side of the rich, the war makers, the racists, the fossil-fuel industry, the multinational corporations, the global surveillance industries, the nuclear weapons manufacturers. God wants catastrophic climate change.

In fact, now we know—there is no God.

That, dear friends, is the voice of despair, the voice of the culture of violence and war, the voice of the fossil-fuel industry, the one percent elite, the Pentagon, the corporations, the war makers, those who practice violence. They do not know the Creator, the God of peace. They have yet to make the beatitude connection Jesus made long ago between nonviolence and the earth. Few have. That is why our theology and spirituality are so skewed, and our faith and nonviolence so weak. We listen not to the God of peace and her glorious creation but to the culture of violence and war and its corporate media. We believe their lies and seal our own doom.

Catastrophic climate change is the ultimate wake-up call. It summons us to change our lives, deepen our nonviolence, listen to creation, reach out to one another, and embark on a new global solidarity. That means we become contemplatives of nonviolence who are in process of inheriting the earth.

Along the way, we are rethinking our theology and spirituality and discovering the underlying theology and spirituality of nonviolence that tells us that we are all one with one another, and all the creatures and Creation itself. Perhaps finally we are learning the true nature of God as a God of peace and nonviolence, as the Creator who freely gave us this beautiful creation as the ultimate gift, who is so nonviolent that she gives us free will to reject God, hurt one another, and destroy this gift. Gandhi said we need to reimagine the nonviolence of God so that we can begin at last to worship a God of peace and nonviolence, and then become a people of peace and nonviolence. Every religion at its roots espouses this theology and spirituality of peace and nonviolence. Catastrophic climate change is forcing us to grow up, adapt this mature theology and spirituality, and protect Mother Earth and her creatures.

"The universe unfolds in God, who fills it completely," Pope Francis tells us. "Hence there is a mystical meaning to be found in a leaf, in a mountain trail, in a dewdrop, in a poor person's face. The ideal is not only to pass from the exterior to the interior to discover the action of God in the soul, but also to discover God in all things."[1] That ideal has become my day-to-day journey.

Many religious leaders and thinkers around the world are beginning to make new connections between the spiritual journey and Mother Earth, as Pope Francis has done. Many books, teachings, retreats, and prayers now point to a whole new spiritual awareness and consciousness—that our journey with the God of peace and one another happens here on earth and cannot be separated from earth. The minute we disconnect from Mother Earth, we disconnect from ourselves, our own spiritual journey, from one another, and from God.

"The world is not a problem to be solved; it is a living being to which we belong," Llewellyn Vaughn-Lee writes in his anthology *Spiritual Ecology: The Cry of the Earth*, a beautiful collection of interfaith essays by some of our greatest spiritual writers on the environment and climate change.[2] "The world is part of our own self," he continues, "and we are a part of its suffering wholeness. Until we go to the root of our image of separateness, there can be no healing. Only when our feet learn once again how to walk in a sacred manner, and our hearts hear the real music of creation, can we bring the world back into balance."

Scott Brown, author of *Active Peace,* wrote me recently along these lines, suggesting that the way forward is through "healing the belief in separateness, the belief that we are separate from one another, from other species and Earth, from God, that we are separate from anything! Our own healing is not only not separate from the greater healing, it is the most radical ingredient we can contribute. When love is directed at healing the belief in separateness, then we have something! Then, there is hope that is grounded—grounded in action and good psychology and truly transformative energy. If the underlying beliefs don't change, then the systems created by those beliefs won't change either. We may go part way but we won't go all the way.

"Interbeing is the truth," Scott continued. "The work, the practice, is simply to become more and more conscious of this. This is where mindfulness comes in as the most basic and fundamental of practices. Naming the belief in separateness as the root cause and bringing attention to healing it is an essential step in our survival. Understand the root cause and we know what we are really up against. The insanity isn't 'out there' in the form of bad people and corporations; it's everywhere and it includes us. We're embedded in this too. No separation. We tend to want to think we're separate from pipelines and oil spills and those systems but we are not. Looking deeply at this, facing the truth that there is no quick fix, the grief flows naturally, the humility rises organically, self-righteousness disappears. It comes from the heart and not the head. Living from this truth thickens the plot and helps us understand in a more profound way than ever why we need to come together." For Scott, personal healing, societal healing, and ecological healing are the one path before us, a mindful, global journey of healing.

"The bells of mindfulness are sounding," Buddhist Zen master Thich Nhat Hanh adds in *Spiritual Ecology*. "All over the earth, we are experiencing floods, droughts, and massive wildfires. Sea ice is melting in the Arctic and hurricanes and heat waves are killing thousands. The forests are fast disappearing, the deserts are growing, species are becoming extinct every day, and yet we continue to consume, ignoring the ringing bells.

"We need a collective awakening," Nhat Hanh continues. "Most people are still sleeping. We all have a great desire to be able to live in peace and to have environmental sustainability. What most of us don't yet have are concrete ways of making our commitment to sustainable living a reality in our daily lives. It's time for each of us to wake up and take action in our own lives. If we awaken to our true situation, there will be a change in our collective consciousness."

"The dream of an infinitely expandable planet placed entirely at our disposal was always just that, a dream, and it's fast becoming a nightmare," Zen teacher Susan Murphy adds in *Spiritual Ecology*. "Tumultuous change on a vast scale grows increasingly likely with every day of business as usual. The only question is what form it will take, which order of climate shocks and political crises will start to shake our world apart, and how people will react as the market collapses and the source of plenty evaporates.

"We are living in what must surely be the most daunting and arresting moment we have ever faced as a species," Murphy continues. "We face a developing reality that can either condemn human beings to oblivion or inspire us to wake up to our lives in a dramatically more interesting way. A way that begins in living soberly and creatively toward the crisis of our planet—

not as a problem to be solved by engineering an ever better, safer human 'bubble,' but as a constantly unfolding obligation to begin considering the remaking of ourselves as ecologically awakened human beings. When the stakes are life on earth, all else is a diversion."

"We are moving from an era dominated by competing nation states to one that is birthing a sustainable multicultural planetary civilization," Mary Evelyn Tucker and Brian Swimme write.

"There can never be world peace as long as you make war against Mother Earth," Chief Oren Lyons of the Onondaga Nation writes. "To make war against Mother Earth is to destroy and to corrupt, to kill, to poison. When we do that, we will not have peace. The first peace comes with your mother, Mother Earth."

"I don't know what is going to happen," Sister Miriam MacGillis, a Catholic nun, longtime environmentalist, and founder of Genesis Farm, confesses. "It's a great sorrow. Letting the pain of this into one's psyche—it's a lot. What we're doing to each other, and whether we can possibly wake up in time. . . . You must do your little part, and you've got to be very, very humble and realize that there are limitations. And yet the love that I experience for life—I just want it to go on! That's all I care about.

"The Earth is going through terrible devastation, which is being caused by the society, and culture, and a way of life we are all implicated in," she continues. "We're not redeemed out of this. We're implicit, we're in it. We need all the wisdom, all the support we can get. We need each other. We also need the capacity to see that the present moment is not the final word, that there is always the possibility that we can transcend our own limitations—the planet, the Earth, the society can do that. It's possible to believe that and work toward it. That's all we can do."

"The earth and its life systems, on which we all entirely

depend (just like God!), might soon become the very thing that will convert us to a simple lifestyle, to necessary community, and to an inherent and universal sense of reverence for the Holy," Franciscan Father Richard Rohr writes. "We all breathe the same air and drink the same water. There are no Jewish, Christian, or Muslim versions of these universal elements."

"I know it is no longer words, doctrines, and mental belief systems that can or will reveal the fullness of this Cosmic Christ," he concludes. "This earth indeed is the very Body of God, and it is from this body that we are born, live, suffer, die and resurrect to eternal life. Either all is God's Great Project, or we may rightly wonder whether anything is. At the level of survival we are fast approaching, our attempts to distinguish ourselves by accidental and historical differences and theological subtleties—while ignoring the clear 'bottom line'—are becoming an almost blasphemous waste of time and a shocking disrespect for God's one, beautiful, and multitudinous life. I do still believe that grace is inherent to creation, and that God and goodness will still have the final word."

Vaughn-Lee ends his collection with a prayer: "May we remember our role as guardians of the Earth, custodians of its sacred ways, and return once again to live in harmony with its natural rhythms and laws."

That prayer, that hope, and that mission have now become a new interfaith, interbeing, common calling. The common ground of interfaith, interbeing nonviolence, we now know, is literally the ground we walk.

CHAPTER 13

The Call of Pope Francis

In the spring of 2016, eighty stalwart Catholic peacemakers from over twenty-five nations were invited to the Vatican for the first ever conference to discuss formally abandoning the so-called just war theory and formally returning the church to the nonviolence of Jesus. This was the first ever gathering of its kind in church history.

For three days, we deliberated at the Vatican about questions of violence, war, and nonviolence. Catholic peace leaders came from Iraq, Afghanistan, Palestine, the Democratic Republic of the Congo, South Sudan, Kenya, Uganda, Colombia, Guatemala, Mexico, the Philippines, and Japan. Everyone who attended had submitted a paper ahead of time about their vision of peace and nonviolence as well as their own experience living and practicing nonviolence, often in war zones. We shared our stories, reflected on the nonviolence of Jesus, and talked passionately about throwing out the "just war" theory, and calling for a new "just peace" paradigm. During the last closing hours we discussed and debated a draft of a statement, which was eventually completed, approved, and released the following day at a press conference at the Vatican radio.

What is so unusual about this development is that it was cosponsored and hosted by the Vatican Pontifical Council for Justice and Peace. We were welcomed by the head of the council, Cardinal Peter Turkson, who was the leader behind

Laudato si', Pope Francis's recent encyclical on the environment. Nine of his staff attended the conference. Turkson opened the conference by reading a long letter of welcome from Pope Francis, and sat in during the final hours as we debated the wording of the conference statement. He gave his full support to the conference and the statement, which, in the end, called on Pope Francis to write a new encyclical that would formally reject the just war theory once and for all and return the church to the nonviolence of Jesus.

This had never happened before. With this event, this statement, and this call, the church could change course after 1,700 years of supporting warfare and killing. A new encyclical on nonviolence could open up a whole new history for Christianity and return us to the spirit of the early church, where no one was allowed to participate in war, prepare for war, or kill another human being, where everyone had to practice and teach the nonviolence of Jesus. Coming in the wake of the pope's encyclical on the environment, it would link the Beatitude of Jesus and help humanity to connect the life and vision of nonviolence with care for creation.

The statement, called "An Appeal to the Catholic Church to Re-Commit to the Centrality of Gospel Nonviolence," offers four points: first, that Jesus was meticulously nonviolent; that there is no just war and we should never again invoke the so-called just war theory; that nonviolence as a methodology for positive social change works, whether in our personal lives, in nations, and internationally, that it can resolve conflict and peacefully transform any situation; and, finally, that the time has come for the church to apply nonviolence at every level around the world.[1]

I was asked to speak to the group about Jesus and nonviolence. That's easy, I said: Nonviolence is the only thing Jesus ever taught. He did not teach us how to kill or wage war or make money; he taught us how to be nonviolent, love our enemies, and make peace. In the Sermon on the Mount, he says: "Blessed are the peacemakers, they are the sons and daughters of God." "You have heard it said, thou shall not kill; I say to you, do not even get angry: be reconciled." "You have heard it said, an eye for an eye but I say to you, offer no violent resistance to one who does evil. . . . Love your enemies." These core teachings forbid all violence, including participation in the mortal sin of war. Nowhere does he say: "but if your enemies are really bad, and you meet these seven conditions, kill them." There is no just war; there are no exceptions. We are not allowed to kill. Period.

For the nonviolent Jesus, there is no cause however noble for which we support the taking of a single human life, much less thousands or millions. He calls us to pursue the endless creativity of nonviolence. What's even more exciting is that he commands us to love our enemies because we really are sons and daughters of the God who lets his sun rise on the good and the bad and the rain to fall on the just and the unjust. In other words, God is nonviolent.

While I was attending the Vatican Conference on Nonviolence, our host, Cardinal Peter Turkson, asked me to write a draft of the 2017 World Day of Peace address on nonviolence for Pope Francis. I sent him a draft, as did my friends Ken Butigan of Campaign Nonviolence and Marie Dennis of Pax Christi International. On January 1, 2017, we were glad to see our main points, even some of our exact language, included in the document, "Nonviolence—A Style of Politics for Peace." It was the first statement on nonviolence in the history of the Catholic Church—since the Sermon on the Mount

The pope's concluding words are a source of consolation as well as a challenge for us in the days ahead:

> Active nonviolence is a way of showing that unity is truly more powerful and more fruitful than conflict. Everything in the world is interconnected. Differences can cause frictions, but let us face them constructively and nonviolently.
>
> I pledge the assistance of the Church in every effort to build peace through active and creative nonviolence. Every

such response, however modest, helps to build a world free of violence, the first step towards justice and peace. May we dedicate ourselves prayerfully and actively to banishing violence from our hearts, words and deeds, and to becoming nonviolent people and to build nonviolent communities that care for our common home.[2]

The Pope's Historic Call to Protect Mother Earth

"Faced as we are with global environmental deterioration, I wish to address every person living on this planet." That's how Pope Francis begins his extraordinary 2015 encyclical *Laudato si': On Care for Our Common Home*. It is a plea for humanity to wake up, serve the Creator and creation, and end the environmental destruction that threatens creatures, ecosystems, and humanity itself. Citing various church documents, biblical references, scientific research, and the lives of Jesus and St. Francis of Assisi, he calls us to become stewards of Mother Earth, to care for this great gift, and to spend our days at one with creation. It is a stunning, original, timely, and magnificent testament, worthy of our study.

And yet, it has been widely ignored, first of all, by priests, bishops, and ordinary Catholics in North America. The general silence about this prophetic text speaks volumes. They do not like this progressive pope, nor do they intend to take seriously his call for solidarity with the earth. And it is a call. Francis summons us to an "ecological conversion," a "loving awareness that we are not disconnected from the rest of creatures, but joined in a splendid universal communion."[3]

After he published his encyclical, Pope Francis came to the United States, met with President Obama, addressed Congress, and overnight brought with him a fresh new spirit of peace, hope, and reconciliation, a spirit that has been widely missing. By the end of 2015, when environmental and government leaders met in Paris at COP 21, the first global breakthroughs on the environment began to happen. Actor Robert Redford, a longtime environmentalist, attributed the hopeful change to Pope Francis.

"I think the thing that was probably a game changer—because those voices were so loud in Congress—was when Pope Francis came to the United States," Redford told the *New York Times*.[4] "When he spoke, he put climate change up front, and he talked about it being a moral issue, not a political issue. When he did that, I think right away it pointed an arrow at the negative part of politics playing a role in climate change. . . . The American Congress is just too polarized. It's stuck. It's not serving the people. So he went outside that. When he did that, it drew attention to the issue, so it's finally beginning to really move."

"God does not only give us life," Francis says, "he gives us the earth, he gives us all of creation. He also gives human beings a task, he gives them a mission. He invites them to be a part of his creative work and he says: Cultivate it! I am giving you seeds, soil, water, and sun. I am giving you your hands and those of your brothers and sisters. There it is, it is yours. It is a gift, a present, an offering."[5]

"Living our vocation to be protectors of God's handiwork," Francis says, "is essential to a life of virtue. It is not an optional or a secondary aspect of our Christian experience."[6] That essential characteristic of Christian life—as protectors of God's handiwork—has to become a new vocation for everyone, if we are to survive.

Care for Our Common Home: An Urgent Encyclical on Behalf of the Planet

"This sister cries out to us because of the harm we have inflicted on her by our irresponsible use and abuse of the goods with which God has endowed her," Francis starts off, speaking of Mother Earth. "We have come to see ourselves as her lords and masters, entitled to plunder her at will. The violence present in our hearts, wounded by sin, is also reflected in the symptoms of sickness evident in the soil, in the water, in the air and in all forms of life. This is why the earth herself, burdened and laid waste, is among the most abandoned and maltreated of our poor; she 'groans in travail' (Rom 8:22). We have forgotten that we ourselves are dust of the earth (cf. Gen 2:7); our very bodies are made up of her elements, we breathe her air and we receive life and refreshment from her waters."[7]

Francis holds no punches. "These situations have caused sister earth, along with all the abandoned of our world, to cry out, pleading that we take another course. Never have we so hurt and mistreated our common home as we have in the last two hundred years. Yet we are called to be instruments of God our Father, so that our planet might be what he desired when he created it and correspond with his plan for peace, beauty and fullness. The problem is that we still lack the culture needed to confront this crisis. We lack leadership capable of striking out on new paths and meeting the needs of the present with concern for all and without prejudice towards coming generations. The establishment of a legal framework which can set clear boundaries and ensure the protection of ecosystems has become indispensable, otherwise the new power structures based on the techno-economic paradigm may overwhelm not only our politics but also freedom and justice."[8]

"What kind of world do we want to leave to those who come after us, to children who are now growing up?" Francis asks. But then he argues that this question should lead us to question the meaning of life, the presence of God, and the reason for our existence. "When we ask ourselves what kind of world we want to leave behind, we think in the first place of its general direction, its meaning and its values. Unless we struggle with these deeper issues," Francis continues, "I do not believe that our concern for ecology will produce significant results. But if those issues are courageously faced, we are led inexorably to ask other pointed questions: What is the purpose of our life in this world? Why are we here? What is the goal of our work and all our efforts? What need does the earth have of us? It is no longer enough, then, simply to state that we should be concerned for future generations. We need to see that what is at stake is our own dignity. Leaving an inhabitable planet to future generations is, first and foremost, up to us. The issue is one which dramatically affects us, for it has to do with the ultimate meaning of our earthly sojourn."[9]

The way we treat the earth and respond to catastrophic climate change, Francis suggests, reveals the depth of our spirituality, our very humanity. Instead of mistreating the earth and denying the crisis, we should dig deeper spiritual roots, reclaim our humanity, protect Mother Earth, and spend our lives in loving service and peace toward one another and creation. In that light, Francis suggests that catastrophic climate change can become an opportunity, a moment of global spiritual awakening when we all decided to become who we were created to be and to protect creation.

Francis's Solution: Universal Solidarity, Social Love, Political Action

"We must regain the conviction that we need one another, that we have a shared responsibility for others and the world, and that being good and decent are worth it," Francis declares. "We have had enough of immorality and the mockery of ethics, goodness, faith and honesty. It is time to acknowledge that light-hearted superficiality has done us no good. When the foundations of social life are corroded, what ensues are battles over conflicting interests, new forms of violence and brutality, and obstacles to the growth of a genuine culture of care for the environment."[10]

With that, Francis proposes a solution: *We require a new and universal solidarity.* He quotes the bishops of southern Africa:

"Everyone's talents and involvement are needed to redress the damage caused by human abuse of God's creation." "All of us can cooperate as instruments of God for the care of creation, each according to his or her own culture, experience, involvements and talents," Francis tells us.[11]

Francis calls us to "social love." "Love, overflowing with small gestures of mutual care, is also civic and political, and it makes itself felt in every action that seeks to build a better world. Love for society and commitment to the common good are outstanding expressions of a charity which affects not only relationships between individuals but also macro-relationships, social, economic and political ones. That is why the Church set before the world the ideal of a 'civilization of love.' Social love is the key to authentic development. . . . Social love moves us to devise larger strategies to halt environmental degradation and to encourage a 'culture of care' which permeates all of society."[12] This universal solidarity and social love require concrete steps, and he goes on to name a few:

> Education in environmental responsibility can encourage ways of acting which directly and significantly affect the world around us, such as avoiding the use of plastic and paper, reducing water consumption, separating refuse, cooking only what can reasonably be consumed, showing care for other living beings, using public transport or carpooling, planting trees, turning off unnecessary lights, or any number of other practices. All of these reflect a generous and worthy creativity which brings out the best in human beings. Reusing something instead of immediately discarding it, when done for the right reasons, can be an act of love which expresses our own dignity.[13]

"You are called to care for creation not only as responsible citizens, but also as followers of Christ!" Francis told thousands of young people in the Philippines. "Respect for the environment means more than simply using cleaner products or recycling what we use. These are important aspects, but not enough. We need to see, with the eyes of faith, the beauty of God's saving plan, the link between the natural environment and the dignity of the human person. As stewards of God's creation, we are called to make the earth a beautiful garden for the human family. When we destroy our forests, ravage our soil and pollute our seas, we betray that noble calling."[14]

"The time to find global solutions is running out," Francis said after issuing the encyclical. "We can find appropriate solutions only if we act together and in agreement. There is therefore a clear, definitive and urgent ethical imperative to act. An effective fight against global warming will be possible only through a responsible collective action which overcomes particular interests and behaviors and develops unfettered by political and economic pressures. A collective response which is also capable of overcoming mistrust and of fostering a culture of solidarity, of encounter and of dialogue, capable of demonstrating responsibility to protect the planet and the human family."[15]

Since he became pope, Francis has pleaded with the whole world to become people of mercy, loving servants to the poor, and protectors of creation. In Assisi he cried out, "I repeat with all the strength and meekness of love: let us respect creation, let us not be instruments of destruction!"[16] Like the rest of us, he is realizing that this also means becoming people of gospel nonviolence.

Trusting in the Creator, Come What May

As the most widely respected religious leader in the world, who passionately calls us to stop our destruction of the environment and protect creation, Francis urges us to have faith in God, to trust the Creator, and to abide by the boundaries of creation by caring for our common home. "The Creator does not abandon us," Francis concludes. "He never forsakes his loving plan or repents of having created us. Humanity still has the ability to work together in building our common home."[17] "God offers us the light and the strength needed to continue on our way. In the heart of this world, the Lord of life, who loves us so much, is always present. He does not abandon us, he does not leave us alone, for he has united himself definitively to our earth, and his love constantly impels us to find new ways forward."[18]

In that spirit of trust and hopefulness for our Creator, Francis concludes his encyclical with a prayer that we can all take to heart.

> God, you are present in the whole universe and in the smallest of your creatures. You embrace with your tenderness all that exists. Pour out upon us the power of your love, that we may protect life and beauty. Fill us with peace, that we may live as brothers and sisters, harming no one. O God of the poor, help us to rescue the abandoned and forgotten of this earth, so precious in your eyes. Bring healing to our lives, that we may protect the world and not prey on it, that we may sow beauty, not pollution and destruction. Touch the hearts of those who look only for gain at the expense of the poor and the earth. Teach us to discover the worth of each thing, to be filled with awe and contemplation, to recognize that we are profoundly united with every creature as we journey towards your infinite light. We thank you for being with us each day. Encourage us, we pray, in our struggle for justice, love and peace.

CHAPTER 14

Mother Earth Rules

If we are to heed the call and live in true solidarity with Mother Earth for the rest of our lives, then we have to make some changes. Maybe not everything, but certainly some things. This, I figure, is doable. We can choose to live on earth in peace and do our part to stop the destruction of the environment and her creatures for future generations. Why not?

Our time on earth is short. Soon we will return to earth and embark on the great spiritual journey to meet the Creator face-to-face. We don't want to appear before the Creator having spent our lives squandering creation, supporting systemic injustice, and practicing violence. We want to abide by the rules of nonviolence set down by Jesus in the Sermon on the Mount, and spend the days we have remaining serving others, disarming the world, and walking gently on earth so that our Creator will be pleased. We want to leave the lightest footprint as possible on the planet.

Legend holds that when the Buddha walked on earth, his footsteps were so gentle and peaceful that lotus flowers sprang up in his wake. His footsteps actually healed the earth and bore good fruit. The same could be said of the nonviolent Jesus. We want to live so that the same could be said of us.

Guidelines for Living in Solidarity with Mother Earth

As I consider my own journey, the nonviolence of Jesus, the call of Pope Francis, the example of so many heroic peacemakers and environmentalists, as well as the global predicament we face, I imagine that we are called to live by a new set of rules—Mother Earth's rules—guidelines originally set by the Creator that run throughout the Bible and the scriptures of the world's religions as well as the lives of the saints. Let me outline a few to help us on our way as we start a new path walking on earth, protecting the earth, and pursuing a future of nonviolence.

Grief as a New Daily Spiritual Practice

At the beginning of the Sermon on the Mount, just before Jesus connects nonviolence with oneness with the earth, he encourages those who are poor in spirit and those who grieve. Blessed are those who mourn, he says; they shall be comforted. As we witness the drastic effects of climate change, war, and systemic injustice, we can be overwhelmed with emotion. We can become numb, afraid, or angry.

Anger is easy. We can all be angry. We can stew and fume and take out our rage on those around us but that does nothing to advance real positive nonviolent social change. Indeed, Jesus suggests that our anger holds the kernel of violence, that there is a better way to energize, mobilize, and sustain our positive action for nonviolent change. That's through love. But in such a global crisis, in the face of total violence, love requires grief.

So Jesus advises us to grieve. As people of nonviolence, we recognize that every human being is our sister and brother, so we grieve at their suffering and the unjust deaths of millions of sisters and brothers from war, poverty, relievable disease, and environmental destruction. Since many of us were taught not to grieve, this has to become a new spiritual practice. We need to take quiet time and sit in the beauty of creation in the presence of the Creator and grieve. We grieve for our sisters and brothers, for the death and extinction of billions of creatures, and for Mother Earth herself. We feel the pain, let our hearts be broken, move deeper into compassion, and stand up publicly determined to take nonviolent action for justice, peace, and creation.

Grief has to become a normal spiritual practice for us in the difficult years ahead. The more we take formal time to quietly grieve for suffering humanity and suffering creation, the more nonviolent and compassionate we will become, and the more empowered we will be to take public action for justice and peace. This is the teaching Jesus gave just before he spoke of the connection between nonviolence and oneness with creation.

Our attitude will be that of the nonviolent Jesus as he approached Jerusalem at the end of his long public campaign of nonviolence. When he saw the city, Luke reports, he broke down weeping, saying, "If this day you had only known the things that make for peace . . . but alas, it is hidden from your eyes."

These days, we too weep with Jesus as we realize that Jerusalem has become the world. Like Jesus, we will try to learn the things that make for peace, and like Jesus, we will go forth and take public action for justice and peace, as he did in the Temple. But first, we weep.

Daily Meditation and Prayer

Taking time to grieve the deadly effects of climate change and practicing nonviolence in solidarity with Mother Earth require spiritual discipline. If we want to carry on in peace, we need to spend quality time with the Creator in daily meditation and prayer, and become as rooted as possible in God's peaceful presence. If we take time to dwell in love and peace every day with our loving God, not only will we discover greater peace, we will receive new energy to carry on God's peacemaking work on behalf of creation and humanity. It's the encounter with the God of peace that will strengthen us to make peace with others and with creation.

A good practice is to set a definite time, like twenty or thirty minutes each morning, and stick to it. You shut your door, sit down straight, close your eyes, center yourself in peaceful silence, and ask the God of peace, the nonviolent Jesus, and the Holy Spirit to come upon you, to be with you and touch you. I recommend asking for the graces you need, telling Jesus what's in your heart and soul, and then listening attentively as he speaks to your heart. God certainly wants to be with you, love you, heal you, disarm you, and bless you. If you give God permission, God will send you on a mission of peace and non-violence to heal others, including Mother Earth. This seems to be the way God works.

The key is your relationship with God. As with any healthy, loving relationship, you need to spend regular time with the one you love, to abide in each other's presence. It's no different with God. God is waiting for us to come and be with God, but we prefer to do anything but that. We could go through an entire lifetime avoiding God, and God will suffer and wait patiently for us to turn to God.

If instead we place ourselves in the presence of God, at the disposal of God, we will discover God's unconditional love and peace, and find a way to live life in that spirit of unconditional love and peace, so that we might share that gift with others and die in that same spirit of unconditional love and peace. Daily meditation and prayerful peace become the bedrock of our lives. They mark how we live and breathe, how we treat others and walk on earth, how we reach out in service and resist evil, and how we make peace until the day we die.

Through daily meditation and prayerful peace, we can know and be known by the Creator, and find our rightful place in creation, as stewards of Mother Earth, peacemakers in a world of war, people of gospel nonviolence leading others out of the dark culture of violence into the light of peace.

Be as Gentle, Nonviolent, and Compassionate as Possible

To live the beatitude connections of Jesus, we have to go as deep into nonviolence as Jesus. So, we try to be nonviolent and gentle to ourselves, to let ourselves off the hook, to be merciful and kind to ourselves, even to make friends with our-selves. We practice nonviolence with ourselves. We don't beat ourselves up for our mistakes. We learn, reflect, return to the peace of God, and let go of our inner violence, resentments, and hurts. We tend to our own wounds and treat ourselves kindly so we don't wound anyone else. The more we can be gentle, kind, and nonviolent to ourselves, the more we will be able to be gentle, kind, and instinctively nonviolent to others, including all creatures and creation.

This inner work of nonviolence will lead us easily to the outer, public work of nonviolence and connect us with cre-ation. Along the way, without our knowing it, we may become Bodhisattvas of nonviolence and compassion, who give our lives for humanity and creation.

Activists and church people, in particular, need to be atten-tive to their inner and outer nonviolence. Activists tend to be aggressive, angry, bossy, and pushy. I know that from having met thousands of them, and I find all that violence in myself as well. If we want to advocate, promote, and teach nonviolence, we have to practice it meticulously within ourselves and among our relationships and in every aspect of our lives. Church peo-ple, too, tend toward self-righteousness, hunger for power, and glaring hypocrisy. Church people who follow the nonviolent Jesus have to speak the truth with love on the one hand, but also model his humility, poverty of spirit, and broad gentleness every step of the way.

Mindful Living in the Present Moment of Peace with Creation

To grow in deeper, loving awareness of our sisters and brothers, the beautiful creatures, and wonders of creation, we practice the art of mindfulness. That means we try not to live in the past or stew over the future. We give ourselves to the present moment of peace and return to the gentleness of our breath as a way to return to the present moment, the eternal now. The Buddhists teach mindful living, mindful eating, mindful walking, mindful working. Every moment becomes an opportunity to step into the present moment of peace.

"We are speaking of an attitude of the heart," Pope Francis writes, "one which approaches life with serene attentiveness, which is capable of being fully present to someone without thinking of what comes next, which accepts each moment as a gift from God to be lived to the full. Jesus taught us this attitude when he invited us to contemplate the lilies of the field and the birds of the air, or when seeing the rich young man and knowing his restlessness, 'he looked at him with love' (Mk 10:21). He was completely present to everyone and to everything, and in this way, he showed us the way to overcome that unhealthy anxiety which makes us superficial, aggressive and compulsive consumers."[1]

Putting on the mind of the nonviolent Christ and practicing his nonviolence, we learn to contemplate the lilies of the field and the birds of the air. When he rose from the dead, he gave his friends the gift of resurrection peace, breathed on them, and said to receive the Holy Spirit. He sent them on a global mission of peace and nonviolence. We try to follow Jesus by welcoming that gift of resurrection peace, breathing in his Holy Spirit, and walking in his footsteps in his kingdom of nonviolence.

In that mindfulness, everyone shines like the sun. We recognize every human being as a sister and brother, every creature as a gift from God, and Mother Earth as a treasure to be honored and cared for. We too learn to walk mindfully on earth in the present moment of peace. As we do, we not only non-cooperate with injustice and environmental destruction, model gospel nonviolence, and seek justice and peace for everyone, we help everyone step into the present moment of peace, the kingdom of God. Along the way, we discover that we have already entered eternal life. Eternity has begun. We are here, on earth, in the peaceful presence of the Creator.

Be Not Afraid, Cultivate Fearlessness

Prayer, nonviolence, and mindfulness heal us, disarm us, and strengthen us for the journey. In the presence of the God of peace, as we dwell in God's unconditional, nonviolent love, all our fears evaporate. We discover that we need not live in fear anymore. The days of fear and its deadly consequence of selfishness, narcissism, and violence are coming to an end. In this new spirit of fearlessness, our hearts widen to love everyone everywhere with God's unconditional nonviolent love. We even love, respect, and care for all creatures and creation.

The culture of greed and war tells us to be afraid. We hear it on the news, from the president, generals, and weapons' manufacturers. They stir up fear, create fear, name those we should fear, and institutionalize fear. We, on the other hand, ignore all these lies. We pursue the truth that every human being is our very sister and brother, that everyone is lovable, that everyone is called to live in the boundaries of nonviolence, and that the only way to help others is by setting asides our fears and reaching out in nonviolent love toward one and all.

We know that our survival is guaranteed, so we do not fear anyone, or even fear death. We become like Jesus and Gandhi— fearless practitioners of nonviolence who give our lives for suffering humanity and creation, come what may. We willingly give our lives for humanity and creation. As we open more and more into fearless, selfless, all-inclusive, nonviolent love, we become one with Mother Earth and realize our true identities as sons and daughters of the Creator. In this way, we take positive action to protect creation and her creatures for future generations.

Let Go and Walk Forward with an Open Heart

These simple practices help us to become our true selves, to be more human. To be our true self we have to let go of everything that is false, every illusion, untruth, desire, possession, or attachment. Every day, we let go of everything we cling to. Over and over, we let it all go, live within the boundaries of nonviolence, and step into the new freedom of boundless peace.

This is how Jesus lived. St. Paul wrote beautifully of Jesus' *kenosis*, his self-emptying love, his continuing to let go until he emptied himself completely on the cross. He did not cling to anything or anyone. He let go of anger and fear; he did not fight or retaliate, he dwelt in the present moment of peace, filled with the peace of God. He embodied nonviolence.

We can do the same. We too learn to let go and practice daily emptiness so that we live nonviolently, reclaim our humanity, feel empathy, and show compassion for others. Letting go simplifies our lives, makes us real, modest, and humble and allows us to be vulnerable, despite the myth of power and domination. The culture of war and domination always promotes power and strength as the ideal. This power-over-us is central to the culture of violence and destruction of the earth. It only brings death and destruction. Instead, we were created to be vulnerable, nonviolent, and peaceful. We come into the world as a vulnerable, nonviolent, powerless baby, and we live the world in that same vulnerable, nonviolent, powerless state. In our vulnerable humanity is the power of nonviolence, compassion, and love.

Jesus shows us that vulnerability and weakness hold real strength and power. Jesus was vulnerable and open, even unto death, and became a spiritual explosion of nonviolence. Vulnerability leads to true nonviolence and opens us to the power of love and peace that can work through us to disarm the world, heal humanity and creation, and restore us all to right relationship.

My friend Roshi Joan Halifax points out that the culture of violence and war teaches us to have a strong front, and does not care about our weak back. She calls us, instead, to carry a "soft front" and maintain a "strong back." We let go, empty ourselves, allow God to disarm our hearts, offer our hands to others and creation, surrender our lives to the universe and so live in a posture of openness. Through our vulnerable opening to others, we continually open our hearts to everyone and all creation, and walk forward in peace with everyone everywhere. We are so open, we even let go of the fruit of our action, giving our lives for nonviolent action for creation and suffering humanity, but not clinging to the results so that all results lie in the hands of the Creator. Along the way, we discover divine peace, surrender to universal love, and enter eternal life.

Contemplative Listening and Nonviolent Communication

"If we can learn to listen to the land," Terry Tempest Williams writes, "we can learn to listen to each other." Contemplative nonviolence means learning to listen to creation, to one another, and to the Creator. We enjoy the peace of silence as we await the inner voice of love to speak a word of love to us. We smile at others and listen to them with peace and openness. We help one another to become more nonviolent, to practice nonviolent communication with one another, and to learn to live in nonviolent relationship with one another.

On this journey of nonviolence, we open ourselves to all others, all creatures, creation, and the Creator, and find ourselves delving deeper and deeper into peace. We even experience moments when we become peace. This daily practice of peace requires relationship with everyone and all of creation, and requires an attitude of nonviolence in every aspect of relationship.

Our contemplative listening, nonviolent communication, and mindful living help us to become nonviolent people who walk gently on earth and treat others gently so that peace can spring forth around us. Our own nonviolent behavior can inspire others to live more nonviolently and makes it easier for others to realize that someday everyone could agree to the boundaries of nonviolence and live a nonviolent life.

Loving Service, Generous Giving, and Engaged Global Solidarity

Our openness to God, one another, creatures, and Mother Earth leads us to widen our hearts and surrender our lives more and more to God, our sisters and brothers, and creation. We learn to give our lives for others, to spend our days not in selfish pursuit of money or security but in loving service of suffering humanity and Mother Earth. We realize that we are at one with everyone, with all creatures and all creation, and we want to remain in this spiritual oneness, to live in that unity always. That leads us to give ourselves over and over again to that oneness, to the Creator and creation.

From now on, we live in global solidarity with all 7.2 billion people, doing what we can to help end human suffering, lead others to the limitless boundaries of nonviolence, and work for a new culture of nonviolence, justice, and peace. We engage in global solidarity with all creatures and Mother Earth, too, so we put our lives, our hearts, and our bodies at their service. We do our best to serve humanity and creation without a trace of the desire for reciprocation because we love everyone and all creation and have been touched by a loving creation, and realize this is the greatest thing we can do for our lives.

Become Vegetarians

If you want to be a peacemaker, you will want to eat as peaceful a diet as possible, Leo Tolstoy wrote. "Vegetarianism," he said, "is the taproot of humanitarianism." Great humanitarians such as Mahatma Gandhi, Albert Schweitzer, and Thich Nhat

Hanh agree. The only diet for a peacemaker, for an environmentalist, is a vegetarian diet.

"Not to hurt our humble brethren, the animals," St. Francis of Assisi said, "is our first duty to them, but to stop there is not enough. We have a higher mission: to be of service to them whenever they require it. If you have people who will exclude any of God's creatures from the shelter of compassion and pity," he continued, "you will have people who will deal likewise with other people." Gandhi put it this way: "The greatness of a nation can be judged by the way its animals are treated."

I became a vegetarian thirty-five years ago, after reading Frances Moore Lappé's book *Diet for a Small Planet*, which makes an unassailable case that vegetarianism is the best way to eliminate world hunger as well as to sustain the environment. A hundred million tons of grain go yearly for biofuel—a morally questionable use of foodstuffs. But more than seven times that much—some 760 million tons, according to the United Nations—goes into the bellies of farmed animals, this to fatten them up so that sirloin steaks, hamburgers, and pork roasts grace the tables of First-World people. It boils down to this. Over 70 percent of U.S. grain and 80 percent of corn are fed to farm animals rather than people. This is an environmental disaster.

Conscience dictates that the grain should stay where it is grown, from South America to Africa. And it should be fed to the local malnourished poor, not to the chickens destined for our KFC buckets. The environmental think tank, the Worldwatch Institute, sums it up: "Continued growth in meat output is dependent on feeding grain to animals, creating competition for grain between affluent meat eaters and the world's poor."

Meanwhile, eating meat causes almost 40 percent more greenhouse-gas emissions than all the cars, trucks, and planes in the world combined. The world's 1.3 billion cattle release tons of methane into the atmosphere, and hundreds of millions of CO_2 molecules are released by forests that are burning because of dry conditions as in California or because of purposeful burns to create cow pastures in Latin America.

And global warming isn't the only environmental issue. Almost forty years ago, Lappé spelled out in stark relief the environmental consequences of eating meat. More recently, her analysis received some high-power validation. The United Nations recently published *Livestock's Long Shadow*. It concludes that eating meat is "one of the most significant contributors to the most serious environmental problems, at every scale from local to global." And it insists that the meat industry "should be a major policy focus when dealing with problems of land degradation, climate change and air pollution, water shortage and water pollution, and loss of biodiversity."

Much of our potable water and much of our fossil-fuel supply is wasted on rearing chickens, pigs, and other animals for humans to eat. And over 50 percent of forests worldwide have been cleared to raise or feed livestock for meat eating. (A recent protest in Brazil denounced Kentucky Fried Chicken for clearing thousands of acres of untouched Amazon rain forest for chicken feed.)

Vegetarian diets avoid the chemicals in meat, help keep our weight down, support a lifetime of good health, and provide protection against numerous diseases, including the three biggest killers in the United States—heart disease, cancer, and stroke. But our appetite for meat leads to widespread, horrific cruelty to animals—chickens pressed wing-to-wing into filthy sheds and debeaked, for example. And since I've always espoused creative nonviolence as the fundamental gospel value, my vegetarianism helps me not to participate in the vicious torture and destruction of billions of cows, chickens, and so many other creatures.

These chickens never raise families, root in the soil, build nests, or do anything natural. Often, they are tormented or tortured before they are slowly killed—as PETA has repeatedly documented in its undercover investigations—for your chicken dinner or hamburger. Animals have feelings, they suffer; they have needs and desires. They were created by God to breathe fresh air, raise their families, peck in the grass, or root in the soil. Today's farms don't let them do anything God designed them to do. Animal scientists attest that farm animals have personalities and interests, that chickens and pigs can be smarter than dogs and cats. I like that even Jesus identified himself as "a mother hen who longs to gather us under her wings."

"When our hearts are authentically open to universal communion, this sense of fraternity excludes nothing and no one," Pope Francis writes. "It follows that our indifference or cruelty toward fellow creatures of this world sooner or later affects the treatment we mete out to other human beings. We have only one heart, and the same wretchedness which leads us to mistreat an animal will not be long in showing itself in our relationships with other people. Every act of cruelty toward any creature is contrary to human dignity. We can hardly consider ourselves to be fully loving if we disregard any aspect of reality. . . . Everything is related, and we human beings are united as brothers and sisters on a wonderful pilgrimage, woven together by the love God has for each of his creatures and which also unites us in fond affection with brother sun, sister moon, brother river and mother earth."[2]

I admire the Bible's greatest vegetarian, Daniel, the nonviolent resister who refused to defile himself by eating the king's meat. He and three friends became healthier than anyone else through their vegetarian diet. And they excelled in wisdom, for "God rewards them with knowledge and skill in all learning and wisdom."

It is also important to remember that the Bible begins with a vision of paradise, the Garden of Eden, where God, animals, and humans recreate in peace together. Clearly, the Bible calls us to return to that paradise. And from the beginning, God directs us to be vegetarians. Genesis 1:29 states, "See, I give you every seed-bearing plant all over the earth and every tree that has seed-bearing fruit on it to be your food."

In the book of Isaiah, we're offered a vision of reconciled creation, a new nonviolent world when "the wolf shall be a guest of the lamb, and the leopard shall lie down with the kid; the calf and the young lion shall browse together with a little child to guide them. The cow and the beast shall be neighbors, together their young shall rest. The lion shall eat hay like the ox. The baby shall play by the cobra's den and the child lay his hand on the adder's lair. There shall be no harm or ruin on all my holy mountain, for the earth shall be filled with knowledge of the God of peace, as water covers the sea" (Isa. 11:1-9). Isaiah lifts up the possibility of a nonviolent world, where all people and all creatures are nonviolent. He calls us to pursue that peaceful vision in every aspect of our lives, from the jobs we hold, to our use of renewable energies, to what we eat and wear, say and do. For me, it is the only vision worth pursuing.

A one percent reduction in worldwide meat intake has the same benefit as a $3 trillion investment in solar energy.

If you are serious about caring for the environment, you have to become a vegetarian.

Recycle; Avoid Plastics; Go Solar

Right environmental practice starts where we are, with what we eat, what we wear, how we live, who we think we are. The basic household steps include installing new environmentally sound light bulbs in our home, office, school, and church; recycling everything we can with meticulous care; eating locally grown organic foods; composting; paying attention to our use of water; reducing our water use; reducing our carbon footprint; driving less, walking and biking more; planting trees and a garden; and financially supporting local and global environmental groups and movements.

In particular, I urge everyone to stop using disposable plastic as much as possible. Somewhere in the Pacific Ocean, a mound of plastic—twice the size of Texas—is floating around, poisoning and killing fish and sea creatures. That mound will continue to grow and destroy life as we continue our senseless use of plastic, which never really goes away and eventually ends up inside our fish and creatures. We need to stop our reliance on plastic as much as we can. Every one of us can take concrete daily steps to do this. My friend Jackson Browne once said he eliminated all plastic from his home—even finding an alternative way to package shampoo.

We also need to support alternative sources of energy, especially solar energy. We might not all be able to live off the grid, though I urge everyone to give it a try, but we can all try to transfer our energy source to solar. We can install solar panels in our homes, offices, schools, and churches. We will save money in the long run, inspire others by our environmental spirit, and do our small part to reduce our reliance on fossil fuels. Germany hopes to go completely solar in a few years; we need to do our part, too.

Build Community, Practice Hope

We can't do any of this on our own. If we try to take a stand against the culture of violence and climate change on our own, we will quickly give up. What we need are people committed to the nonviolent struggle *for life*. That means, we have to make a new commitment to one another.

Systemic violence is bigger than any of us. Saint Paul states flatly that what we are up against is not just a dictator, tyrant, or narcissistic sociopath, but the structures and institutions of death, "the principalities and powers," he calls them. We need the support and strength of other committed people to help us remain committed, to maintain our spirit and struggle, and to generate hope within and among us. Otherwise, we'll end up watching on CNN the bombs fall and saying to ourselves, "That's too bad; if only someone could have done something." Then, we become the passers-by at Calvary, who walk past the crucified Jesus saying, "That's too bad; if only someone could have done something." We don't want to be passers-by who lament the killing of sisters and brothers around the world and the destruction of Mother Earth saying, "If only somebody could have done something." We want to do something, and there's plenty to do, so let's get on with it. But the best way to take positive action for creation is with others. Together, in community, in a movement, more gets done, hope gets generated, and victories are won.

The first thing Jesus did was to form a community. Mahatma Gandhi, too, formed a community in South Africa and went on to live in an ashram for almost fifty years. Since the 1970s, hundreds of thousands of base communities sprang up across the impoverished villages of Latin America, where ordinary, disenfranchised people met to pray, read the scriptures, share together, strategize for hope, build movements for justice and peace, and take action. Those base communities were key to the historic national transformations that took place in the 2000s. Africa and Asia likewise became home to countless base communities.

As the United States moves deeper into fascism, permanent war, total surveillance, and corporate greed, as catastrophic climate change bears down upon us, we too need to form and join local base communities where we pray, read the scriptures, study the issues, share our pain and hopes, build the global movement, and take action. In that way, through our local peace group, environmental group, church group, or affinity group, we can contribute to the movements and find the strength to stay with the struggle throughout our lives. Plus, we'll make new lifelong friends who share our vision.

My friend Daniel Berrigan worked for peace until his death at age ninety-four. But what many don't know is that besides living in a community of priests, he belonged to a small, local New York City peace community that met every other Tuesday evening since the late 1970s. It's still going. I was part of that group for over twenty years. We prayed, shared reflections, plotted some public work for disarmament and justice, and supported one another to stay with the struggle. The support we gave each other helped everyone to spend their lives working for justice and peace, Dan included.

In the process, we found hope. We gave each other hope. When someone was particularly discouraged or filled with despair, another person could present reasons for hope and for carrying on despite the evidence. That's how nonviolence works—when people continue to work for justice, disarmament, and creation—and even though they know they might not live long enough to see the positive changes they want, and they keep on working anyway, then the conditions are set for nonviolence to become contagious. Over time, more people join the movement. If people stay with it, and do one or two or three tasks a day, eventually the tide turns and the transformation begins. Community helps us sustain the struggle, strengthen our long-term commitment, and build the movement. As Thich Nhat Hanh once said to me, "Everything I have done is because of my community. You can do more with a community."

Martin Luther King Jr. defined hope as "the final refusal to give up." Together, we refuse to give up and do what we can for justice, disarmament, and creation, come what may. That, I believe, is the will of God for us in these times—the willingness to keep at it whether we succeed or not; the willingness to be faithful to the wisdom and way of nonviolence as our life, spiritual path, and common future; the willingness to keep at it come what may, even that final refusal to give up. In the end, our lives and bodies become seeds of transformation and new hope.

Join the Global Grassroots Movement; Take Public Action for Climate Justice

"We don't have to engage in grand, heroic actions to participate in the process of change," Howard Zinn once wrote. "Small acts, when multiplied by millions of people, can transform the world."

If humanity is to have a future of peace, everyone must get involved. We don't have to do grand gestures, as Howard Zinn tells us; we just have to do our small, daily, ordinary part. As Archbishop Romero said on the day he was assassinated, "Nobody can do everything, but everyone can do something." That must become our mantra—keep engaging in strategic, nonviolent, public action for justice, disarmament, and creation, no matter what. It has to become an ordinary part of our lives from now on.

Through our participation in grassroots movements, we can help resist and stop systemic environmental destruction, permanent war, and corporate greed. We can defend life, protect creation, model nonviolence, and make a big difference. We have more power than we realize.

After thirty-five years' full-time involvement with these movements, I have found, however, that some risk, some personal sacrifice, some gift of ourselves is required for positive social change. We really do have to give of ourselves and make the movement, not money or possessions, a priority in our lives. Some of us engage in nonviolent civil disobedience and face the possibility of prison for justice and peace, as Gandhi and King did. If we want to participate on the front lines of the global movements, in militant nonviolence as Gandhi described it, we should. Just go forward as prayerful, mindful, conscious, and nonviolent as possible.

Whatever we do, it is crucial that we do something on behalf of Mother Earth, her creatures, and suffering humanity. Giving up, giving in, sitting back, doing nothing, wallowing in despair, burning in anger, helps no one, certainly not Mother Earth. Get with a group of people you can pray with and march with, Daniel Berrigan advised, and start praying and taking public action for justice and peace.

Teach Nonviolence Far and Wide, Especially to Priests and Ministers

I invite everyone to talk about nonviolence with everyone around them from now on—to your parents, children, relatives, neighbors, coworkers, religious leaders, politicians, police, and community members. I think we need to take nonviolence into the mainstream, and start a national and international conversation about the meaning and vision of nonviolence, how we can become more nonviolent, and what steps we need nationally and internationally for the coming of a more nonviolent world. That means we all need to become students and teachers of nonviolence, in the tradition of Gandhi and Dr. King. It's the most important topic on the planet, it should be our number one topic of discussion, but it's the one thing we do not discuss.

In particular, it would help if we engaged our local priests, ministers, and religious leaders in a dialogue about creative nonviolence. Ninety-five percent of them have never heard a word about nonviolence and don't know that Jesus was nonviolent; they can't teach it because no one has taught them. Each one of us has to start teaching our priests, ministers, and religious leaders the wisdom and way of nonviolence. We can visit with them, give them books, ask them about Jesus' nonviolence, and discuss the Beatitudes and the Sermon on the Mount with them. We can lead them away from the just war theory and any support of violence, war, or nationalism, from their fear and silence about teaching nonviolence, and welcome them into the universal nonviolence of Jesus as a new way of life for them and everyone. I suggest we undertake a one-on-

one campaign to convert every religious leader in our community to the wisdom of gospel nonviolence. Most especially, we need to convert North American Christians to the nonviolence of Jesus. That long-haul work of education and transformation will one day bear good fruit—literally, in the protection of creation—if we each do our part.

Undertake Constructive Programs for a New Eco-Sustainable Culture of Nonviolence

Gandhi insisted that creative nonviolence was not just about resisting systemic violence and injustice but advocating and promoting a new culture of nonviolence here and now, usually through small grassroots projects that model the nonviolent society we aspire to. That's why throughout the Indian resistance to British imperial domination, he advocated spinning cloth every day on a spinning wheel as a practical task for every Indian to withdraw from the British cloth industry and jump start a national Indian cloth industry, if just a local cottage industry. He built an ashram, developed schools and food services, called for the reform of the Hindu religion, supported a new and equal role for women in society, and by and large modeled in his own life and community the kind of nonviolent India he envisioned. He would want us to do the same.

As we build and organize a national and global movement of nonviolence to resist environmental destruction and the corporate greed and militarism that maintain it, we can also begin local, national, and international constructive programs that help us become the kind of nonviolent people and societies we envision.

There are countless kinds of constructive programs we can join—from the Nonviolent Cities project, to local community centers, school and after-school programs, women's programs, low-income housing, community-based financial coops, food coops, organic farms, interfaith networks, and local coop health care programs. But there are even more countless constructive programs yet to be envisioned and enacted. Through our part in a constructive program, each one of us can learn not just to say No to the culture of violence and injustice but Yes to a new culture of nonviolence and justice.

Cultivate Childlike Wonder and Gratitude, Rejoice in Creation

It's not all grim. As we pray, practice nonviolence, live mindfully in the present moment, and build up the global grassroots movements to protect Mother Earth, we can take time every day to appreciate the wonders of creation as never before. Along with the grief we feel, we can cultivate daily gratitude and childlike wonder for Mother Earth, her creatures, and all creation. This will unleash a new, long-buried inner joy. Like St. Francis, we too praise the Creator for Brother Sun and Sister Moon, enjoy the song and flight of birds, contemplate the beauty of flowers and every growing thing, and marvel at the ocean, the mountains, and the stars. Mother Earth becomes our Temple, and every sentient being a sign of a loving Creator. We return to our original childlike wonder and make that disposition a new way of life. We give thanks and take heart in the beauty that surrounds us and reclaim an inner joy that no one will take from us again.

"Inner peace is closely related to care for ecology and for the common good because, lived out authentically," Pope Francis writes, "it is reflected in a balanced lifestyle together with a capacity for wonder which takes us to a deeper understanding of life. An integral ecology includes taking time to recover a serene harmony with creation, reflecting on our lifestyle and our ideals, and contemplating the Creator who lives among us and surrounds us."[3]

I've tried to maintain that childlike wonder and joy all my life, even when in prison or in war zones. I love people, love children, and love the elderly, and I've always loved animals and the wonders of the world. When I was six, I wrote a book about animals. I cut out a hundred color pictures of animals from the countless magazines my parents had, pasted each one on a piece of colored paper, and wrote a few sentences about each one. In high school, for my physics class project, I wrote a long paper about clouds and the science, math, and weather behind them. That meant I got to spend many long hours lying on the ground looking up at the passing clouds.

I've traveled the world, speaking about peace and working for peace, and everywhere I've gone, I've taken time to get out and walk mindfully amidst the wonder of creation. I held a koala bear in Australia, stood before a herd of zebras and elephants in South Africa, watched a whale breech near our boat off the coast of Maui, ridden horses since childhood, surfed almost every ocean, swam with dolphins and turtles, hiked deserts and mountains, and witnessed countless sunsets. These miraculous sights and experiences have left me in awe, filled me with wonder, and turned me from despair and darkness back to joy and gratitude. They remind me how small we are in the great universal scheme of things, and lead me to praise the Creator for such gifts. They teach me that I am not in charge, that our Creator is good and has lavished us with undeserved spectacular gifts, and that it is not a burden at all to do our little part on behalf of Mother Earth, her creatures, and our suffering sisters and brothers.

Appreciation of Mother Earth, her creatures, and the glories of the universe is the job of every human being. We were created to live nonviolently in peace with one another on Mother Earth and celebrate the beauty of creation morning, noon, and night.

From now on, we seek to restore this Garden of Eden, protect her for future generations, and give thanks to the Creator for such a gift.

From now on, every day is Earth Day.

CHAPTER 15

Blessed Are the Nonviolent: They Will Live in Peace with Mother Earth

It's common on North Carolina's Outer Banks to see pelicans glide effortlessly in single file a foot above the breaking waves along the coastline. On occasion, I've seen a hundred pelicans circle over a dark area in the ocean, then dive, one by one, straight down into the water to feed off a school of fish.

The other day I watched in wonder as a dozen dolphins swam by. I especially enjoy studying sandpipers, the small, white birds with tiny legs like toothpicks who run down the beach right into the face of an oncoming wave, pick at the sand, and then turn around and run back before they get hit by the wave. Back and forth, all day long, they run right into the face of an oncoming wall of water and then turn around. The oncoming tsunami does not seem to terrify them, but what a way to spend one's life!

The North Carolina coast is known for its rugged beauty and raw wildness. It's a good place to step out of our violent, consumer society and rediscover the refreshing reality of creation. Because the Outer Banks jut far out into the Atlantic, the currents and tides are particularly rough. The ocean can seem enchanting one day, and angry and menacing the next. It is alive, and one feels more alive in its presence.

I was born and raised not far from Nags Head, and I return here periodically, to the place of my childhood, to refresh myself in the beauty and wonder of creation. I've been coming here all my life and feel at home on these dunes, by these roaring waves, under this big sky, in the company of pelicans, dolphins, and sandpipers.

During the 1960s, since we lived close by, we visited the beach regularly. For two or three weeks each summer, we rented one of the classic flat-top houses and spent our days in the water—literally. My three brothers and I, along with our father, would run into the ocean at 8 a.m. and get out at 5 p.m. every day for the entire two or three weeks. We were fish. I was permanently sunburned but didn't care. We thought everyone did this. At night, we went go-cart racing. Those were some of the happiest days of my life.

These days, I prefer the off season when only the locals can be found at the coffee shop. Before the Cineplex, McDonald's, and Walmart, back in the 1960s, the Outer Banks were barren. The sand dunes of Jockey's Ridge could be seen for miles, just as they had been fifty years before when the Wright Brothers first flew across them. The only stores around were Wink's and Anderson's, in a tiny cinderblock building that sold everything. Twenty miles south near the bridge to Manteo and Roanoke Island stood the little yellow Holy Trinity Catholic Church at Whalebone Junction. Not far north stood the beautiful old Currituck lighthouse. No one had a telephone, a TV, a computer, or air conditioning. It was stark, simple, primeval, but quiet, healing, and peaceful.

At night, standing alone on the quiet beach, I look up and see the stars and watch the moonlight shimmering on the rolling ocean and listen to the sound of crashing waves. There's not a soul in sight, and the ocean stretches out far until it merges with the night sky. Here, one sees the big picture. Everything points to God. Everything bears God's fingerprints. Everything makes sense, makes peace.

In the morning, I'm up early to catch the sunrise over the ocean. Light appears along the horizon, a few clouds turn pink, then red. Suddenly, a red line appears and then the sun pops up and I see the light. I walk two miles down the beach to the Avalon Pier and find the local fishermen and women standing above on the pier or knee deep in the water with their fishing rods. I think of those comforting words, "Come, follow me and I will make you fishers of men and women." I recall how the Galileans dropped their nets and walked off with Jesus.

But that's not how it feels this morning. It feels, on second thought, like the journey has come to an end, and not just my journey, but in the face of catastrophic climate change, creation's journey. It feels like we are witnessing the crucifixion of Mother Earth. I feel like St. Peter after Jesus' arrest and execution, at a loss to understand our ongoing rejection of peace, love, and nonviolence. Peter goes back to Galilee and starts all over again. He takes out a boat and goes fishing, and the others join him. That's all they know how to do.

Like Peter, I'm back where I started. And here, by the sea, at dawn, the risen Jesus approaches with his Easter gift of peace and says, as if for the first time, "Peace be with you. As I was sent, so I send you. Come, follow me" (John 21).

Once again, I hear the call to take up the journey. It's like I'm always beginning. And the initiative always comes from God. As we keep watch over the world with its wars, corrupt governments, greedy corporations, stupid racism and sexism, extreme poverty, unjust suffering, nuclear weapons, and environmental destruction, we trust in the God of peace and keep going forward into ever-widening peace with all humanity, all creatures, all creation, and the Creator.

It's in those moments under the night sky, by the sea, or before the rising sun, as we remember the essential truths and our great calling, as we take heart from the growing movements for climate justice and peace, as we practice mindfulness and open ourselves to the Great Compassion, as we reach out in loving kindness and creative peacemaking, that we take heart once again and step forward to follow the nonviolent Jesus as he goes ahead of us.

For Christians, the best way forward in these scary times, perhaps the only way forward, is to keep our hearts and minds and our eyes set on the nonviolent Jesus at all times, come what may. Jesus embodies nonviolence and the campaign for a nonviolent world. He walked the earth, formed a nonviolent grassroots movement of steadfast resistance to imperial domination and systemic injustice, and gave his life to that nonviolent campaign. He lived at one with humanity and creation, in perfect love and peace; but as far as the culture of greed and war was concerned, he failed completely. He was betrayed by a member of his community, which then abandoned him and left him to face arrest, torture, and public execution alone.

And yet, the story does not end there. Reports began to circulate that he was alive, that he had returned as nonviolent as ever, and that he called his friends to "follow him" all over again, to carry on his mission of creative nonviolence to the ends of the earth.

That mission continues today. We are part of it. We, too, might be "holy failures," but we are summoned to a great spiritual undertaking—to carry on Jesus' campaign of nonviolence for justice, disarmament, and Mother Earth and to enter the promised land of peace by living at one with humanity and creation.

Like the nonviolent Jesus, we need to trust in God and maintain our faith even in the darkest hour. We do this through daily prayer and meditation, daily Gospel reading and regular communal worship. As servants and friends of Jesus, we live like him, speak like him, resist systemic injustice like him, and love humanity and Mother Earth like him. We stay centered in the God of peace, and live in the Spirit of God, and so walk the earth in universal love, compassion, and peace.

"The one who becomes a friend of God," Pope Francis writes, "loves his brothers and sisters, commits himself to safeguarding their life and their health, and also to respecting the environment and nature."[1] Since we keep our eyes on Jesus, we join his campaign of nonviolence and follow him as he goes ahead of us to Jerusalem, even to the cross of nonviolent resistance to systemic injustice and environmental destruction. We are willing to share his paschal mystery as the way to human and global transformation. We pray for, proclaim, and welcome God's kingdom of peace and nonviolence on earth. In a spirit of peace, come what may, we do our little part to live out this mission and keep it alive.

Jesus practiced what I call "eschatological nonviolence." When he walked gently on earth, he was walking as if he was living fully in the kingdom of God, right now, here on earth. That meant he had all the time in the world to be present, loving, and peaceful. There wasn't a trace of violence in him. He called us to do the same later in the Sermon on the Mount, when he taught us to "seek first the kingdom of God." That's eschatological nonviolence.

Eschatology is the study of the "last things," the "end times," "the end of the world." More, it's the study of the beginning of eternity—the end of time and the beginning of eternity, the start of eternal life and the coming of heaven on earth, all rolled into one. According to Jesus' visionary nonviolence, everyone will eventually convert to nonviolence and everyone will welcome God's reign of nonviolence here on earth. In this light, Gandhi concluded that when everyone finally does embrace and adopt the wisdom of nonviolence, God will rule on earth exactly as God rules in heaven.

With eschatological nonviolence, we too focus on the kingdom of God. We pray for it, imagine it, and look for it. We ponder, imagine, and welcome God's reign as that new realm without war, destruction, or death. We try to act from now on as if we are already there. We live and breathe and walk as consciously, mindfully as we can, here and now, as if we are already in the fullness of the kingdom of God—because in fact, we are!

This kind of wild visionary thinking gets laughed at, but this is what the nonviolent Jesus taught, and what Pope Francis now calls us to practice. For me, this is the spiritual life. In light of catastrophic climate change, it has to become the basic teaching and common practice of every human being. Everyone is called to live their lives right now in the kingdom of God, to practice now as if they were already in the fullness of the presence of the God of peace. As we do, we will reject every form of violence, from war and executions to racism and sexism to nuclear weapons and corporate greed to destructive behavior to the creatures and Mother Earth. Nonviolence will be the new normal, the accepted boundary line of all human behavior, a new law of nature. We will train every human being in the methodology of nonviolence so that everyone knows how to respond to conflict nonviolently, resolving it without hurting others. The causes of war would one day be rooted out, justice will flourish for everyone, Mother Earth and her creatures would be protected, and war will be a thing of the distant past. That is the vision of eschatological nonviolence.

This, I submit, is our new common vocation—to break beyond the narrow nationalistic identities imposed upon us by nations, cultures, militaries, and their media, and to claim our true identities as children of Mother Earth and the Creator, at one with every human being, every creature, and even the air, water, and land. From now on, like the nonviolent Jesus, we practice eschatological nonviolence, and walk on earth as if we are in the kingdom of God.

From now on, we are one with creation and the Creator, and we act like that. We accept the social, economic, racial, political, and environmental implications of eschatological nonviolence. We practice the global politics of nonviolence and support the global grassroots movements of nonviolence. In this way, we begin to inherit the earth, and fulfill the beatitude teachings of the nonviolent Jesus.

In other words, we are called to become people of "total nonviolence"—to go as deep into nonviolence personally, communally, and globally in every aspect, in every way, from now on as far and as wide as possible! Our basic prayer is for humanity's conversion to "total nonviolence." This is exactly what the nonviolent Jesus taught his disciples to pray for in the Sermon on the Mount: "May your kingdom of nonviolence come, your will of nonviolence be done, on earth as it is in heaven. . . ."

From now on, we are universal people who live in universal communion, people who practice universal nonviolence, universal love, and universal peace. It's as simple and as difficult as that.

We are in the process of discovering what it means to be the blessed, meek, and nonviolent disciples of Jesus, and so, to inherit the earth. As we strive to live that beatitude connection that Jesus teaches, we become global citizens, universal people, children of Mother Earth and of the God of peace and discover how blessed we already are.

What I'm trying to say is that in the face of catastrophic climate change and global violence, we can give up, give in, and surrender. Once we start on that downward path, we lose our integrity and become our worst selves. But I'm inviting us instead to rise to the occasion and become our best selves! In this grave hour, I encourage us all to become our true selves, to deepen our nonviolence, to become mature disciples of the nonviolent Jesus, to broaden our solidarity with creation and humanity, and to serve the God of peace by protecting Mother Earth and her creatures as best we can until the day we die. This, dear friends, must become our finest hour.

Standing on the wide brown beach at Nags Head, I breathe in the cool fresh air as the waves crash on the shore a few feet away. The sandpipers run back and forth, the pelicans fly along the coastline, and a few other people walk along the beach, and all at once, it feels so easy. We are living in the kingdom of God already. We can be at peace with everyone. Eschatological nonviolence is the way forward; total nonviolence is the new vision; universal nonviolence is the new path, and new hope appears on the horizon as we learn to live at peace with Mother Earth, her creatures, and one another.

It's as simple as breathing in the fresh air, and taking the next step.

Conclusion

It's the morning after the presidential election of Donald Trump, and like billions of people around the globe, I'm saddened by the turn of events. I sit in silent meditation for hours, concentrating on the breath of the Holy Spirit, the presence of the God of peace, my discipleship to the nonviolent Jesus, as I look out the window across the mesa to the distant desert mountains. I remember that it doesn't really matter in the end about particular people, that we are up against the principalities and powers, the culture of war and death itself, that I am a follower of the nonviolent Jesus and trying to live here and now in God's reign of infinite loving nonviolence, and so I return to my center. Eventually, in a spirit of grief, peace, and oneness with Mother Earth, I set off north for several hours to the remote corner of northwestern New Mexico, to Abiquiu and the spectacular red and orange cliffs of Ghost Ranch.

Once the home of the Johnson family and legendary artist Georgia O'Keeffe, Ghost Ranch comprises 21,000 acres of mesas, mountains, canyons, cliffs, and rivers, and is now the national retreat and conference center for the Presbyterian Church, where over three hundred classes are offered each year and dozens of Hollywood blockbusters have been filmed.

It's a perfect, clear blue, sunny day. I park and head down to the stables, where I hire a wrangler, a young woman just out of college, to take me horseback riding for the afternoon. She introduces me to Nacho, a stunning, beautiful, dark-brown stallion with a gentle disposition. I climb on top, grab his mane, stroke his neck, and off we go, as I follow her and her horse, ten yards ahead of me.

For the next two hours, I leave the planet and enter another universe. Or rather, I leave the illusion of television, negativity, and imperial politics and come back down to earth. Nacho and I walk along a thin dirt path through miles of sagebrush, rocks, pinion, pine, and juniper trees, along the foot of the towering red and yellow cliffs made famous by Georgia O'Keeffe, who lived in a little adobe house several miles ahead of us. Ahead and on our left, we can see miles of desert sagebrush with red and orange cliffs and mountains lining the far horizon. In the distance, to the south, the flat-topped Pedernal mountain keeps watch over the entire moonscape. It was this landscape that inspired Georgia O'Keeffe to chart a new course in American painting. She could do so because she became one with this particular piece of earth.

The horse seems relaxed and peaceful, like me and the landscape. We breath in and out, at peace, taking it all in, gently feeling at one with our surroundings, the big sky, the cool breeze, the strange cliffs and exotic mesas and distant vistas. The stupidity of national politics and the possibility of fascism evaporate, and I enter an eternal present moment of peace. It must be the kingdom of God, I tell myself. There is no other way to live, except in this eschatological nonviolence, in this nonviolent end time, this new nonviolent beginning of eternity, beyond the illusion of separation, into the reality of eternal oneness. Nacho and I breathe in, take it one step at a time, sometimes diving ten feet straight down into some hidden arroyo and then just as quickly diving straight up ten feet back to level ground, both of us exhilarated by the geography and journey of peace.

What more could we want than oneness with such creation, with such a creature, with such a universal spirit of peace? This is the calling of every human being—to enter into the universal nonviolence of the present moment, to ground ourselves on

Mother Earth and become one with her, to follow the nonviolent Jesus on his campaign for the coming of God's reign of nonviolence here on earth. We need not get caught up in the winds of culture, the tornado of violence, the tsunami of empire. We can resist, noncooperate, remain centered, be at peace, and honor creation, come what may, until we slip into eternity and our bodies return to Mother Earth from whence they came. In doing so, our lives will bear good fruit.

We will do our part to build up the global grassroots movement of nonviolence on behalf of suffering humanity and creation, so that all may live in peace, that none may come to harm, none may be destroyed, and that God's Garden of Eden will bloom again one day.

This, I realize, is the hidden ground that I will walk on the journey into the promised land of peace.

Nacho stops and looks up. He takes a deep breath and takes in the view, as if he too knows that this is the promised land, that we have already arrived, that we are at home, at one with the here and now.

I give thanks to the Creator for Mother Earth, for the astonishing creatures, for so many beautiful sisters and brothers, and for this present moment of peace. Nacho starts up again.

We keep walking, going forward, taking our time, enjoying Mother Earth, one step at a time. We are all one.

Closing Prayer

Dear God of peace, Creator God,
I pray for Mother Earth. Please intervene and stop our ongoing destruction of the environment, land, water, and air. It's as if we are drunkards heading toward death, oblivious to our actions. The nations of the world seem determined to extract fossil fuels and any resource that will bring more money, regardless of the consequences of our actions upon the earth, the poor, or future generations. At this rate, we will unleash unlimited carbons, raise the earth's temperature, melt the polar ice caps, and unleash catastrophic climate change with unparalleled hurricanes, tornadoes, floods, fires, and droughts, that will kill millions, poison the water, and unleash a global hell of permanent war.

Dear God, prevent us from this ongoing crucifixion of the earth. Help us to stop the destruction of the earth and to be nonviolent to the earth. Give us the wisdom to share the earth together wisely, to protect our water, land, and air, to leave fossil fuels in the ground and pursue alternative forms of energy, such as wind and solar power. Give us an entirely new understanding that we might put Mother Earth and her creatures first, that we might also protect the poor and vulnerable, that we might legislate global protection of the environment and stop greedy corporations from raping Mother Earth and killing her poor.

Creator God, anything is possible with you. We need to be healed, personally, globally, ecologically. We are sorry for our environmental destruction and systemic violence. We grieve the damage and death we have caused. We repent of our environmental violence, our hatred of the poor, of your creatures, of your creation. Our violence is our own self-destruction. We have gone insane. Give us the sanity of nonviolence.

Give us a new will, a new spirit, a new heart, a new grassroots movement to protect creation. Save ourselves through your grace, and help us embark on a new future of nonviolence and respect for creation and one another.

We love you for the gift of your creation, for the beauty of Mother Earth. Thank you for such a gift. Do not let us destroy it. Do not let the nations of the world burn it down, wage permanent war, lead your creatures to extinction, and kill millions of sisters and brothers along the way. Give us the wisdom and way forward, that we might become who you created us to be—your beloved sons and daughters, instruments of your peace and nonviolence, loving stewards of your beautiful paradise. Amen.

Questions for Personal Reflection and Small Group Discussion

What does the third beatitude mean to you? Why does Jesus connect "meekness" (or nonviolence) with inheriting the earth? What is the connection between creative nonviolence and oneness with creation? How can we begin to live this beatitude connection more and more?

How have you moved closer into solidarity with Mother Earth? What concrete steps have you taken (from recycling to changing light bulbs to going solar or moving off the grid)? What new steps can you take?

How can you break through the illusion of our separateness from creation and move deeper and deeper into the reality of our oneness with Mother Earth, all creatures, every human being, and God?

How do you see Jesus as a person of nonviolence who lived at one with humanity and creation itself? As a Christian, what is your responsibility to Mother Earth, her creatures, and suffering humanity? How do you live the teachings of the Sermon on the Mount? What does the nonviolence of Jesus mean to you?

How do you respond to Pope Francis's encyclical *Laudato si'*, and all his impassioned calls to protect the environment, serve the poor, advocate for justice, and practice nonviolence?

How have you been involved with the global grassroots movement of nonviolence to protect creation and her creatures, and what new steps can you take to help build up the global grassroots movement of nonviolence, justice, and peace on behalf of Mother Earth?

Which suggestions in "Mother Earth Rules" did you resonate with, and which ones challenged you? Which ones do you agree with, and which ones do you disagree with? What new steps can you take to join this vision of service on behalf of Mother Earth, her creatures, and humanity?

How can you pursue "eschatological nonviolence"? What would it mean for you to try more and more to live every moment in "the kingdom of God," in the presence of God's peace, and so to practice "total nonviolence"?

How can you teach, discuss, and spread the wisdom and call of gospel nonviolence more and more to those around you— your family and friends, your community and workplace, your priest or minister, your church group or activist group?

What is your vision of a nonviolent future? How can you help your city become a "nonviolent city"? How can you help others pursue a new vision of nonviolence for the world, and do what you can to end environmental destruction and promote right stewardship for Mother Earth? What is the Creator calling you to do on behalf of creation?

Notes

Chapter 4. Walking on Earth Like the Nonviolent Jesus

1. Pope Francis, *Laudato si'*, #97.
2. Ibid., #221.

Chapter 7. Berta Caceres, Martyr for Mother Earth, **Presente!**

1. *Democracy Now*, March 6, 2016.
2. Darryl Fears, "For Latin American Environmentalists . . . ," *Washington Post*, March 30, 2016.
3. Beverly Bell, "The Life and Legacy of Berta Caceres," www.Other WorldsArePossible.org.
4. www.goldmanprize.com.
5. Phone interviews with my friends Jean Stokan and Scott Wright, July 2016.

Chapter 8. Taking a Stand at Standing Rock

1. "Time to Move the Standing Rock Pipeline," *New York Times*, November 3, 2016.
2. Pope Francis, *Laudato si'*, #146.

Chapter 9. A Global Movement for Mother Earth

1. Pope Francis, *Laudato si'*, #14.
2. Bill McKibben, "A Call to Arms," *Rolling Stone*, June 5, 2014.
3. Bill McKibben, "Can Anything Good Come from Climate Change? An Interview with Bill McKibben," *The Plough* (Spring 2015), 13.
4. Ibid., 10-11.

5. Bill McKibben, "Breaking Away from Fossil Fuels," speech in Seattle, WA, April 4, 2016, broadcast on *Alternative Radio.*

6. Ibid.

7. Bill McKibben, "Changing the Rules of Engagement," *Sojourners* (March 2017), 14.

8. Ibid.

9. McKibben, "Breaking Away."

10. McKibben, "Can Anything Good," 13.

11. Bill McKibben, "A Stupid and Reckless Decision," *New York Times,* June 1, 2017.

12. "Donald Trump Is a Disaster for the Earth on Every Single Level: An Interview with Bill McKibben," *Mother Jones* (November 11, 2016).

13. McKibben, "Changing the Rules," 14.

14. Michael Brune, www.sierraclub.org, November 9, 2016.

Chapter 10. Connecting the Dots through Campaign Nonviolence

1. Pope Francis, *Laudato si'*, #94.

2. Ibid., #49.

3. Ibid., *Laudato si'*, #158.

4. Pope Francis, "Caring for Creation," *Franciscan Media* (2016), 87.

5. Ibid., 92.

6. Tamara Lorincz, "Demilitarization for Deep Decarbonization," International Peace Bureau (September 2014), www.ipb.org.

7. Martin Luther King Jr., *A Testament of Hope: The Essential Writings of Martin Luther King Jr.,* ed. James Washington (New York: Harper & Row, 1986), 224-26.

Chapter 12. A Down-to-Earth Spiritual Life

1. Pope Francis, *Laudato si'*, #233.

2. *Spiritual Ecology: The Cry of the Earth,* ed. Llewellyn Vaughn-Lee (Point Reyes, CA: Golden Sufi Center Press, 2013).

Chapter 13. The Call of Pope Francis

1. See www.nonviolencejustpeace.net.

2. Pope Francis, "Nonviolence: A Style of Politics for Peace," January 1, 2017; see www.nonviolencejustpeace.net.

3. Pope Francis, *Laudato si'*, #220.
4. Interview with Robert Redford, *The New York Times,* December 6, 2015.
5. Pope Francis, "Caring for Creation," *Franciscan Media* (2016), 8-9.
6. Pope Francis, *Laudato si'*, #217.
7. Ibid., #2.
8. Ibid., #53.
9. Ibid., #160.
10. Ibid., #229.
11. Ibid., #14.
12. Ibid., #231.
13. Ibid., #211.
14. Pope Francis, "Caring for Creation," 113.
15. Ibid., 164.
16. Ibid., 24.
17. Pope Francis, *Laudato si'*, #13.
18. Ibid., #245.

Chapter 14. Mother Earth Rules

1. Pope Francis, *Laudato si'*, #226.
2. Ibid., #92.
3. Ibid., #225.

Chapter 15. Blessed Are the Nonviolent: They Will Live in Peace with Mother Earth

1. Pope Francis, "Caring for Creation," *Franciscan Media* (2016), 103.

Acknowledgments

My thanks, first of all, to my friends and colleagues at Pace e Bene for their support—Ken Butigan, Ryan Hall, Veronica Pelicaric, Kit Evans-Ford, Rev. Jim Lawson, and everyone in the Campaign Nonviolence movement.

I thank all my friends for their kindness, help, and support, especially Steve Kelly, Danny O'Regan, Mark Deats, Scott Brown, Larry Rasmussen, Mairead Maguire, Natalie Goldberg, Joe Schmidt, Dar Williams, Patty Smythe, Scott Nash, Marian Naranjo, Eric Stoner, Jeff Harbour, Kathy Kelly, Janet and Martin Sheen, Barbara and Jim Reale, Pat and Brian Dear, Helen Prejean, Margaret Maggio, Richard Garcia, Marie Dennis, Bud Ryan, Ellie Voutselas, David and Sharon Halsey Hoover, Anne Symens Bucher, Mark and Carla Berrigan-Pittarelli, Scott Wright and Jean Stokan, Bill McKibben, Ann Wright, Dennis Kucinich, Shirley and Earl Crow, Lee Mickey, Bob Lussier, Desmond Tutu, Ray East, Gerty East, Shelley and Jim Douglass, Patti Normile, John Cusack, Nancy Cusack, Liz McAlister, Carole Powell, Wally Inglis, Chris Ponnet, Joan Baez, Jackson Browne, Joe Sands, Shane Claiborne, Carlos Santana, Tim DeChristopher, Joan Brown, Arun Gandhi, Michael Brune, Terry Rynne, Phil Cousineau, Danny Muller, Joe Cosgrove, Louis Vitale, Gerry Straub, Bruce Friedrich, Janice Vanderhaar, Jim Wallis, Richard Rohr, Kerry Kennedy, Joan Halifax, and Dolores Gardini and David Mark of Yosemite. Special thanks to Connie Clark for all her great editorial suggestions.

Finally, I thank my dear friend and editor, Robert Ellsberg, and Orbis Books for publishing these reflections.

I thank all who work to protect creation, promote nonviolence, and make the connections between justice, peace, and creation. I dedicate these reflections to Renea and Mat, friends and neighbors who share the mesa with me and help me to live at peace with creation.

About the Author

John Dear is an internationally known voice for peace and non-violence. He is a Catholic priest, activist, organizer, lecturer, and author of over thirty-five books on peace and nonviolence. He is on the staff of Pace e Bene, a co-founder of Campaign Nonviolence.org, and part of the Vatican Nonviolence Initiative. He has been nominated for the Nobel Peace Prize many times, including by Archbishop Desmond Tutu. He lives in northern New Mexico. See www.johndear.org.